EXAM *Revision* NOTES

AS

UK ...ent
and

rd Edition

Patrick
Series e...

Philip Allan Updates, an imprint of Hodder Education, an Hachette UK company, Market Place, Deddington, Oxfordshire OX15 0SE

Orders

Bookpoint Ltd, 130 Milton Park, Abingdon, Oxfordshire OX14 4SB
tel: 01235 827827
fax: 01235 400401
e-mail: education@bookpoint.co.uk

Lines are open 9.00 a.m.–5.00 p.m., Monday to Saturday, with a 24-hour message answering service. You can also order through the Philip Allan Updates website:
www.philipallan.co.uk

ISBN 978-0-340-99081-0

First printed 2010

Impression number	5	4	3	2	1
Year	2014	2013	2012	2011	2010

Typeset by Pantek Arts Ltd, Maidstone, Kent

Printed in Spain

Hachette UK's policy is to use papers that are natural, renewable and recyclable products and made from wood grown in sustainable forests. The logging and manufacturing processes are expected to conform to the environmental regulations of the country of origin.

P01782

Contents

Topic 5 Pressure groups

Topic 6 The constitution

Topic 7 The prime minister and cabinet

Topic 8 Ministers and the civil service

Introduction

About this book

Before you use this book you should have already:

- made use of the recommended textbook(s) — try to ensure that you use one which is designed for AS and is not out of date
- made your own detailed notes on all the key topics that form the core of the AS specification
- taken a lot of care to get up-to-date examples of political events for all the topics you are studying in order to get the large number of marks that are allocated to knowledge of contemporary politics
- looked carefully at past AS papers for the exam board you are doing — make sure that they are for the new specification which started in 2009
- looked at the mark schemes (available online), which are what examiners have to follow when they are marking your papers
- practised past papers under timed conditions — this is vital so that you know how much time you have on each question and sub-question (candidates often waste huge amounts of time on questions with few marks and then have too little time to do questions which have a lot of marks allocated)
- checked that you know exactly how marks are allocated in exam papers — how many for factual knowledge and how many for analysis/argument
- checked carefully the specification of the exam board you are doing, which is available online — check that you are doing all the required topics (every year mistakes are made by schools and colleges, so check it for yourself)

All the exam boards publish a lot of useful information on their sites, designed to help teachers and students in Government and Politics. Make use of it.

This book is designed for use as a revision guide to clarify the course, and to prepare you for the AS examination. All the topics listed in the content specification of the three major exam boards are covered here. The layout is designed to enable you to prepare for the types of questions you will get in the two exam papers you have to do. At the beginning of each topic, you will find examples of both short-answer questions and essay-type questions.

About the AS examination

The current regulations for the three major exam boards require AS students to take two AS papers. They are usually between an hour and a quarter and an hour and a half. Fortunately they are no longer on the same day.

Marks are allocated in a straightforward manner, and candidates are well advised to learn carefully exactly how many marks are allocated, and how they are allocated, for each question in each paper. The published mark schemes list the allocation of marks precisely, and this allocation should be carefully noted. One of the reasons why able candidates who know a lot of politics do not do as well as expected is that they simply do not use the required techniques, and so focus their efforts in the wrong way.

AS Government and Politics has three 'Assessment Objectives', and marks are allocated to each of these objectives. The Assessment Objectives are as follows:

- Assessment Objective 1 (AO1) — factual knowledge
- Assessment Objective 2 (AO2) — analysis/evaluation/argument/discussion
- Assessment Objective 3 (AO3) — quality of communication/grammar/spelling/use of appropriate political terms

So a question which has a total of 25 marks might have its marks allocated like this:

AO1   10 marks

AO2   10 marks

AO3   5 marks

The examiner will be expected to put three separate marks at the end of the question, for example: 9/2/4. This shows that the candidate had excellent factual knowledge (9 for AO1), had limited analytic skill or did not bother to answer the question (2 for AO2), and had sound communication skills (4 for AO3). It does not matter how brilliant your argument/analysis is, you can only get 10 marks for it, and if you don't know many facts to back up your ideas then you probably won't get more than an E grade.

In AS you will have three different types of question.

(1) Short-answer questions. These questions are designed to test knowledge and understanding, and are only allocated AO1 marks. The words at the beginning of the question make it clear that only AO1 marks are looked for. They are:
  - **Describe** the role of the cabinet.
  - **Outline** the main features of ministerial responsibility.
  - **What is meant** by pluralism?
  - **Define** representative democracy.
  - **What is the difference between** a political party and a pressure group?
  Usually only 5–10 marks are allocated for these factual questions, so do not spend too much time on them or get involved in a long discussion about the importance or otherwise of the cabinet.

(2) Questions based on sources. These can be looking for both AO1 and AO2. If more than 10 marks are allocated, the examiners want AO2 as well as AO1. You must make use of the sources to get full marks. Again the words at the beginning of the question will tell you whether it is just AO1 marks that are needed. Questions starting in the following ways are only looking for AO1 factual knowledge:
  - With reference to the sources, **outline** the reasons for limiting the power of the prime minister.
  - With reference to the sources and your own knowledge, **describe** the main functions of the House of Commons.

Questions such as the following are looking for both AO1 and AO2 marks (usually split about 50:50), so make sure you earn them:

- With reference to the sources and your own knowledge, **explain why** the House of Lords should be reformed.
- Using the sources and your own knowledge, **discuss** the effectiveness of parliamentary scrutiny of the executive.

Do not forget to make clear use of the sources. Quote from them directly.

(3) **Essay-type questions.** Both AO1 and AO2 marks are allocated for essay questions, usually about the same number of marks to each. The key words in the question that indicate this type of question are shown in these examples:

- **To what extent** are pressure groups a threat to democracy?
- **Evaluate** the need for further reform of the constitution.
- **Analyse** the main factors which limit the effectiveness of Parliament.
- **Make out a case** for and against reforming the electoral system.
- **Discuss the view** that it is easy for UK citizens to gain redress of grievances.

AO3 marks — communication skills

It is depressing when candidates simply ignore the fact that up to 20% of the marks are awarded for AO3. These are easy marks to get if you just take care. If, for example, 6 AO3 marks are allocated to an essay (out of a total of 30), examiners will often start by giving you the full 6 marks and then deduct if:

- your spelling, grammar and punctuation are dreadful
- you did not use the appropriate 'political' vocabulary
- you cannot construct a clear argument
- your overall level of communication is bad

On the whole you have to try quite hard to lose those AO3 marks, but plenty of candidates do.

Ensure you answer the question set, not the one you wish had been set, or the one you answered well in the trial exams. The biggest single reason for poor performance is irrelevance.

Democracy and participation

These two topics are compulsory for Edexcel and AQA, and although they are not specified directly for OCR, knowledge of both is important for Unit 1.

To do well in this topic you need to:
- focus on mastering definitions, getting your own definitions for 'democracy', 'rights' and 'electoral apathy'; use the right words in the right context and get the 'language' of politics right, and apply those definitions in the right context
- get your statistics right and make sure you have an in-depth grasp of the 2005 and 2010 elections
- master the right technique for dealing with the questions that come up

> It is vital that you can define democracy clearly and in different contexts.

Short questions

1 Explain the difference between direct and representative democracy.
2 Define liberal democracy.
3 Why has turnout dropped in UK elections?
4 Explain how the UK could be made more democratic.

Essay questions

5 Discuss the main reasons for the decline in turnout in elections.
6 To what extent is it accurate to call the UK a 'liberal' democracy?
7 Discuss the view that the best way to improve participation in politics is to lower the voting age.
8 To what extent is there a democratic deficit in the UK?

1 Democracy

> Democracy: 'people power', or government by the people for the people.

There is a huge debate about the definition and nature of **democracy**, but there is no need to get involved in this — save that for A2 and beyond. However, you do need to be able to define democracy itself and in certain contexts, and also deal with questions about whether the UK is a democracy or whether our parties or electoral systems are 'democratic' or not. Some of the key elements of, and criteria for, democracy are listed below:
- Consent. Does government operate with the consent of its citizens?
- Choice. Does the electorate get a real choice at election time?
- Responsiveness to public opinion. Does the government really consider the views of the governed?
- Regular elections. Are there sufficient opportunities for the electorate to call the government to account?
- **Participation** by all for all. Can all citizens not only vote but also get involved in the political process — become politicians?

> Political participation: getting involved in politics, either directly through voting and joining a political party, or indirectly through a pressure group such as Greenpeace.

- Freedom, rights, liberty, privacy, equality. Are all these factors — which are vital for democracy to flourish — present?
- Separation of powers. Is there effective separation of powers, so that, for example, the executive cannot dominate the legislature and judiciary?

- Open government. Can citizens easily find out what government is doing on their behalf, who is doing it, and why?
- Government by the majority. Are majority views prevailing (but with sufficient attention paid to the views of the minority)?
- Limited government. Are there clear limits to the power of government?
- Accountability. Is there a proper system for calling the government to account?
- Where sovereignty lies. Does sovereignty lie with the people?
- Rule of law. Are all under the law, including the government?

There is no one obvious 'system' of democracy. There are lots of different types, and they place priority on different aspects of the criteria listed above. The ones you need to know about are listed below.

1.1 Direct democracy

'Direct' democracy is closely related to the historic Athenian/Greek 'pure' model of democracy. It is really only suited to tiny units or states where there are few citizens. Its main elements are:

- direct election of government at all levels
- participation by all, in all decisions
- lots of referendums
- highly localised people-power
- no barriers between citizens and government

You can see why this is not suited to a nation with an electorate of more than 45 million.

1.2 Representative democracy

This is the type of democracy which developed in order to blend the needs of democracy with the reality of a large state where it was impossible for everyone to participate in everything, even if they wished to.

The main elements of **representative democracy** are as follows:
- Elections are held regularly, in which all citizens are entitled to participate and stand for election.
- Elected representatives go to parliament and make decisions on behalf of the electorate. These representatives are responsible to their electorates.
- Sovereignty lies with parliament.
- The government/executive is probably not directly elected.
- There are clear and known limits to government.
- There is political liberty.
- Opposition is legal.

1.3 Liberal democracy

There is widespread disagreement among the experts as to what are the essential features of a **'liberal' democracy**, as opposed to any other type of democracy. Some feel that it is just what is happening now in the 'West', where democracy has adapted yet again to meet contemporary needs — in other words, liberal democracy is what works in a capitalist market society but is still basically democratic. Other criteria for liberal democracy might be:

Sidebar notes:

Make sure you can explain the different types of democracy.

Direct democracy: the system whereby all citizens individually participate in the decision-making process.

Representative democracy: the system whereby elected representatives make decisions on behalf of those who elected them.

Liberal democracy: a representative democracy (of the UK type) in which there is limited and accountable government as well as tolerance and respect for human rights.

- There is genuine pluralism.
- It is a tolerant system, particularly of dissent and minorities.
- There is limited government.
- There is open government.
- There is the rule of law and an independent judiciary.
- There is bicameralism — there are two elected chambers in the legislature, each able to check the other.
- There is real liberty for all, with secret elections, a free press and all the other indicators of a free society.

2 *Democracy in the UK*

Make sure you have thought about how 'democratic' the UK is.

In order to deal with questions on how democratic the UK is, or whether it is a liberal democracy, you will need your own definition of a democracy/liberal democracy. Here are some criteria by which you might answer (there is no right or wrong answer on this one!):

- Are there regular elections and are they 'fair'?
- Is there consent and accountability?
- Are there real limits to government?
- Is there plenty of participation and scope for participation?
- Is there freedom of expression?
- Is there freedom of association?
- Is there a proper separation of powers?
- Do citizens have a right of privacy?
- Is there genuinely open and transparent government?
- Is there the rule of law?
- Is there protection for minorities?

2.1 Criticism of UK democracy

If asked to look at the flaws in the democratic process in the UK, here are some factors you might consider:

- The electoral system. Consider the 'wasted' vote and the percentage of voters who actually turned up to vote Labour (which won) in 2005.
- The level of voter participation/disillusionment. Look particularly at turnout in local and European elections (and consider the impact that local government and the European Union [EU] actually have on our lives).
- The dominant party system. Did voters really have much choice in 2001, 2005 and 2010?
- An elective dictatorship. Look at the power of the prime minister, for example, to go to war in Iraq or change the role of the Lord Chancellor (and the constitution!).
- Whips. Look at the way in which the executive dominates the legislature.
- Lords. Should the unelected (such as Lord Archer and Lord Ashcroft) have any power?
- Civil service power/quangos. Has too much power gone to the unelected and the unaccountable?

- Judicial independence. Has the judiciary changed in social background? Are judges still chosen from a tiny elite group who are too close to government?
- Party power, weakness of party members, party financing. Are parties democratic organisations which give too much power to their leaders and too little to their members, and are financed in an 'undemocratic' way?
- Pressure group power. Do some pressure groups have too much power and too much influence over government?
- Media power. Is too much of the media owned by foreigners who are more interested in profits than in ensuring the proper role of a free press in a democracy?
- The EU. Has too much power gone to unelected and unaccountable commissioners and judges?
- Fusion of powers/lack of separation of powers. Does the executive have too much direct control over the legislature and judiciary?
- Secrecy. Do we really have freedom of information?

2.2 The impact of devolution and the EU on democracy in the UK

Devolution of powers to Scotland, Wales and Northern Ireland has arguably made the UK a more democratic country. Some of the reasons you might consider are considered below.

> Consider whether devolution has made the UK more democratic.

Scotland

- It now has primary law-making powers on most domestic issues, such as health and education.
- It has its own directly elected parliament with fixed terms.
- It has a much more 'democratic' electoral system. On the other hand, Scottish parties are more powerful.
- The Scottish Parliament has some taxation powers.
- There is now local choice in education, housing and healthcare, and the freedom to adapt to local needs.
- It is responsible for its own law and order (subject to the European Court of Human Rights, of course).
- There are fixed-term elections.
- There is a new relationship with voters — a lot of time and effort is spent on consultation.
- There is much more 'open' government. Cabinet minutes are published within days and not kept for 30 years, as is the case for No 10.

Northern Ireland

Devolution was different in Northern Ireland, as a major part of the devolution process was bound up with trying to bring about, and keep, the peace. Devolution has arguably made the situation there more 'democratic' in the following ways:

- The rule of law is gradually being established.
- There is an end of direct rule from London, which was strongly opposed by many Northern Irish citizens.

- There is a very different electoral system, based on proportional representation, which has played a key role not only in ending gerrymandering, but also in ensuring that all sectors of the population are represented.
- There is genuine power-sharing between groups that previously were bitterly divided.
- The Northern Ireland executive has decision-making powers on major domestic issues such as education and policing.
- It has its own democratically elected assembly.
- It has taken great care to ensure there is 'open' government.

Wales

In Wales there was much less enthusiasm for devolution. It was rejected in a referendum in 1979, and the 1997 referendum had a very low turnout, with a tiny majority voting in favour of it. Devolution has arguably made life more democratic for those living in Wales.

- The Welsh Assembly has no taxation powers.
- Proportional representation is used for elections to the Welsh Assembly.
- The executive in Wales has some scope for adjusting the way in which the money granted by London is spent.
- The executive has some discretion over domestic issues, such as education and health.
- Great care is taken to ensure there is 'open' government.

2.3 How to enhance democracy?

A very likely question might be on how the UK system of government could be made more democratic. As always there is no right or wrong answer here, but below are some suggestions you might consider:

- Reforming the electoral system to make it more representative and end such elements as the 'wasted' vote. Possibly lowering the voting age as well, and extending the franchise to recent immigrants.
- Reforming Parliament, and the Lords in particular. Giving elected representatives in the House of Commons more power.
- Reducing executive power generally, and the power of the prime minister in particular.
- Reforming political parties, particularly the question of where power lies in parties, and also reforming the ways in which parties are funded.
- Having more **referendums**.
- Devolving more power, not just to Scotland, Wales and Northern Ireland, but to local government.
- Make enhancing and increasing participation a priority.
- Achieving much more openness in government, and much less secrecy.
- Controlling the influence of pressure groups and effectively regulating them.
- Regulating the press to ensure it plays a better role in a modern democracy.
- Bringing in and enforcing a bill of rights.

Referendum:
the process whereby citizens are asked to decide on an issue, usually by giving a simple yes/no answer.

3 *Participation*

3.1 The participation/legitimacy crisis

The number of people participating in the political process, from its simplest aspect of turning up to vote to getting fully involved in a political party and helping administer it both nationally and locally, has sharply declined in recent years. Many see this as deeply worrying (work out what percentage of the electorate — those entitled to vote — put Tony Blair back in power with a comfortable majority in 2005). Is a government put into power by so few voters really legitimate? Does it have a proper mandate? However, some suggest that this is a sign of a contented electorate.

How many actually participate?
- The general election turnout in 1950 was 84%; by 2001 it had dropped to 59%, but in 2010 it rose to 65%.
- In the local elections turnout was 30% in 2009. It is worth noting that local government has an enormous impact on vital areas such as education, social services and the environment, so it is surprising that so few bother to vote.
- Turnout in the EU elections of 2009 went down to 33%.
- Less than about 5% participate in politics fairly actively.
- About 1% are very active politically.
- Party membership in 2009 was:
  - Labour Party: 166,000
  - Liberal Democratic Party: 60,000
  - Conservative Party: 150,000

A significant minority of the population plays no part at all in political or community life. In some cases this is deliberate **abstention**, but homeless people cannot get on the electoral register and those in prison cannot yet vote.

3.2 Why has participation dropped — especially in voting?

Before 1992, about 75% of those entitled to vote actually voted in general elections. The turnout is always much lower in local elections. The general election turnout dropped to 71% in 1997 and then to 59% in 2001 and 61% in 2005. An increasing number of people, particularly those between 18 and 25, are not even bothering to register to vote. Various reasons are put forward for the 39% who were entitled to vote but did not in 2005:
- Young people are more mobile and do not feel involved in the community where they live.
- Simple **apathy**: only 37% of the 'youth' vote turned out in 2005.
- Some people refuse to vote on principle, as they feel alienated from the whole system. The MPs' expenses scandal and the Byers/Hoon scam did not help.
- Party dealignment — the decreasing identification with a major party has ended much of the traditional party loyalty vote.
- The impact of polls — many voters believed Labour would win easily in 2005, so there was no need for them to vote.
- Too long an election campaign, or too long a build-up (the campaign of 1997 was much longer than usual), means the voters get bored.

Abstention: deliberately not participating or voting when there is opportunity to do so.

Which is the major reason for the decline in turnout, and why?

Apathy: a reluctance to get involved in the political processes or take an interest in politics.

- Similarity of policy between the parties — quite a contrast with 1983, for example, when there was a great policy divide between Labour and the Conservatives.
- Voters who had always supported one party getting angry with that party. Labour had moved to the 'right' in 1997, and some argue that many of its traditional supporters felt it was not socialist enough, and so stayed at home in 2005. Turnout was very low in safe Labour seats. Anger over Iraq and university fees in 2005 also led to many former Labour voters abstaining.
- The class issue — in 2005, 70% of the AB class voted, while 54% of the DE class voted.
- People used to vote out of a sense of duty, but now they tend to vote when they feel it can make a difference.
- Many feel it is easier to get things done by joining a pressure group.
- Basic contentment — with a steady increase in living standards for most citizens, there is no need to vote.
- Negative campaigning — the tendency for politicians to be rude about each other and for the media to focus on political failings does not give an attractive image. Too much 'spin' does not help either.
- The electoral system and the wasted vote — those who live in (allegedly) safe seats and oppose the dominant party in that constituency feel there is little point in going out to vote.
- The registration process is a little bureaucratic, and some fear that it might lead to people being tracked down by the taxman or student loan company.
- Alienation — some people simply feel they have no part to play in society.
- Laziness — some simply cannot be bothered to vote.

Why does it matter if participation drops?

3.3 Reforms to extend participation

Various suggestions have been put forward to encourage greater participation in politics and communities. These include:

- More referendums. These could be on a range of issues, from going to war to local planning decisions.
- Lowering the voting age. Sixteen is being suggested as a 'better' age, but present evidence suggests that the younger you are the less likely you are to vote.
- Compulsory voting. Australia has this, and it appears to work well.
- Digital democracy. Greater use would be made of modern communications for involvement and participation, such as online petitions and voting. However, in recent years experiments in postal voting have led to serious fraud.
- Registration drives. This would involve pushing hard in schools and elsewhere the importance of voting, encouraging people to register, and persuading people that the taxman and the DVLA will not track them down if they do.
- Advertising to vote. Mounting a national campaign prior to elections.
- Personal contact by candidates. The latest research in the UK and the USA indicates that the more candidates get out and knock on doors and make maximum contact with potential constituents, the more people will turn out to vote.
- Education in citizenship. Making it clear in schools and colleges that voting and participation is what any normal person ought to do.

Elections, electoral systems, electoral reform and referendums

'If voting changed anything, they'd abolish it' — Ken Livingstone.

This is a major topic for all exam boards. It is a compulsory topic for both Edexcel and AQA. OCR has elections and electoral systems as optional topics.

To do well on these topics you need to:
- make sure you have a good knowledge of the relevant statistics relating to elections and are able to use those statistics correctly when backing up your arguments
- be able to argue a case well, while at the same time showing awareness of alternative views: these are very discursive topics

> Make sure you have a good grasp of the details of the issues surrounding the UK general election of 2010.

Short questions

1 Who may vote, and who may stand as a parliamentary candidate, in UK general elections?
2 Explain what is meant by a government getting a 'mandate' after an election.
3 Explain how the first-past-the-post system works.
4 Explain how elections to the European Parliament differ from elections to the Scottish Parliament.

Essay questions

5 How democratic is the electoral system in the UK?
6 Make out a case for and against reform of the electoral system in the UK.
7 How strong is the case for further use of referendums in the UK?
8 Discuss the view that proportional representation would be a highly positive reform.

1 UK general elections

1.1 The history of UK elections

> Electorate: all those entitled to vote. Note that in 2001, 59% of the UK electorate voted.

Electing MPs for Parliament goes back many hundreds of years. The first step towards giving all adults the right to vote was made in 1832, when disenfranchised (voteless) middle-class men threatened revolution unless the aristocracy gave them the vote. This meant that the **electorate** (those with the right to vote) went up from 2% to 7% of the adult population. Voting was gradually extended in the nineteenth century to better-off working-class men in 1867 and 1884. Voting was done in secret (1872) and honestly (1883/1885). In 1918, women over 30 and all males got the vote. Women over 21 got the vote in 1928, and the age of voting was lowered to 18 in 1969. The decision to have a first-past-the-post system was taken by the Conservative and Liberal parties in the 1880s and was designed to exclude any radical left-wing party developing.

Franchise: the
right to vote.

Constituency: a
geographical area that
has the right to send
one MP to Parliament.

Strong/stable
government: a strong
government (in the
context of elections)
is one which has a
sufficiently large
majority to get its
manifesto promises
passed into law. A stable
government is one with
a guaranteed majority
which is unlikely to
be overthrown by a
parliamentary defeat.

Coalition government:
a government made up
of two or more parties,
neither of which has a
majority in Parliament.
It is usual for the larger
party to provide the
prime minister/chief
executive but for the
smaller party or parties
to have some key posts
in the administration.

1.2 The franchise in the UK

Now about 99% of the population over the age of 18 are allowed to vote. In the nineteenth century, only property owners were able to vote. Now the requirement is to be a citizen of the UK who has registered and is on the electoral register (list of voters). Until 1949 some people had two votes, if they were graduates or owned a business in a different **constituency** (area which sends MPs to Parliament) from the one in which they lived. Now every voter has only one vote per election. Members of the House of Lords, the royal family, those certified insane and those in prison may not vote. Voting is not compulsory, as it is in some countries.

1.3 Who can be a parliamentary candidate?

To stand for Parliament, you have to be over 21 and a UK citizen. No other qualifications, including educational ones, are needed. Criminals convicted of serious crimes, bankrupts, clergy and some officials, such as judges, may not stand as MPs. There are very tight restrictions (dating back to 1883) on how much can be spent on an election. Several elected MPs had legal proceedings started against them in 1997 for failing to observe the rules about spending, and one was convicted.

1.4 Principles of elections in the UK

Think carefully about what ought to be the principles underpinning, and the purpose of, an electoral system.
● Should the aim be to attain democracy?
● Should the aim be to ensure that every vote carries the same weight?
● Should the electoral system produce a **strong government**?
● Should the aim be to have one party with a majority of the seats in Parliament?
● Should the aim be to produce strong leadership?
● Should the result reflect as accurately as possible the views and opinions of the public?
● Should the aim be to avoid **coalition government** (government by more than one party)?

The election results of 2010 clearly raised many issues about the principles of UK general elections.

1.5 The timing of general elections

The Parliament Act of 1911 states that a general election must be held at least every 5 years. However, prime ministers can hold an election earlier by asking the monarch to agree to one (there is a convention that the monarch always agrees) if they think they have a good chance of winning. In times of crisis, it is possible to postpone an election — this happened in 1915 and 1940, during the two world wars. However, this can only be done if the House of Lords agrees — and it is the only issue over which the Lords have a full veto. Tony Blair held the elections of 2001 and 2005 a year before he had to, because he felt he had a better chance of winning. Gordon Brown decided not to hold an election in 2007,

Fixed-term elections became a major part of the coalition 'deal' in 2010: why?

and this was felt to have been a serious mistake. Some feel that this gives the prime minister too much influence over the result, since he or she can choose the time most favourable to the prime minister's own party. Fixed-term general elections appeared for the first time in party manifestos in 2010 and were part of the 'deal' between the Conservatives and Liberal Democrats in 2010.

1.6 By-elections

By-elections occur when there is a single vacancy in one constituency: for example, when an MP dies. The rules are the same as those for general elections, but there is usually great media interest, and a much higher level of spending by each party is allowed. By-elections can be seen as an important way of gauging public opinion between general elections. Unusually, Tony Blair's governments between 1997 and 2005 did quite well in by-elections, although in many cases the number of Labour voters fell. However, Labour lost four seats between 2005 and 2010, which was seen as damaging to Gordon Brown's authority.

1.7 Local elections

These are fixed-term elections which take place every 4 years. The rules about who may be a candidate in local elections are the same as those for general elections. Like general elections, local elections are usually conducted on party lines, but the turnout is much lower than is the case with general elections: usually less than a third of the electorate votes. In some local elections every councillor is up for re-election every fourth year, while in others some are elected each year — but still for a 4-year term. A first-past-the-post system is used. The supplementary vote system, where the voter has two votes, is used to elect the Mayor of London and other directly elected mayors. Again they have a fixed term.

1.8 European elections

Which system, the Scottish or that used for the EU, can be seen as 'fairer'?

The UK is entitled to send 72 MEPs (Members of the European Parliament) to the European Parliament. There are considerable differences between the ways in which MEPs and MPs are elected. The system used for European elections is a type of proportional representation called the closed-list system. You need to know this system well, and the main differences between it and the system used in general elections in the UK. The main features of the system are as follows:

- It is similar to the system used in other EU countries.
- They are fixed-term elections.
- Voters choose parties and not candidates on their ballot papers.
- Voters vote regionally and not in individual constituencies.
- The UK is divided into 12 regions, and each region, such as the East of England, is given one MEP for every approximately 600,000 voters, and seven seats in total.
- If a party gets 50% of the vote in a region that has four MEPs allocated, it will get two of those seats, and the seats will be given to the first two candidates named on the party's list of candidates for that region.
- The rules about deposits and spending are similar to those for UK elections.
- Turnout is usually about 30%.

Party	Share of the vote	Seats won
Conservative	28%	26
UKIP	16%	13
Labour	16%	13
Liberal Democratic	14%	11
Green	9%	2
BNP	6%	2
SNP	2%	2
Plaid Cymru	1%	1
Sinn Fein	1%	1
DUP	1%	1

Table 2.1 The 2009 European election results for the UK: 72 seats

Party	Share of the vote	Seats won
Conservative	31%	3
UKIP	20%	2
Liberal Democratic	14%	1
Labour	11%	1

Table 2.2 The 2009 European election results for the East of England: seven seats

1.9 Elections for the Scottish Parliament

This is very different from the system used for UK general elections.

- There are 129 MSPs (Members of the Scottish Parliament).
- There are 73 constituencies.
- Each voter has two votes: one for a constituency MSP and one for a party.
- One MSP is elected from each constituency using the simple plurality system used in UK general elections.
- A further 56 MSPs are chosen using a closed-list system very similar to the one described above for European elections — this is where the second vote is used.
- Scotland is divided into eight regions, which are the same as the 'Euroregions'. Each region has seven MSPs and they are elected on a proportional basis. If a party wins 60% of the vote in a region, it will get four of the seven MSP seats allocated to that region.
- They are fixed-term elections — held every 4 years.

Party	Share of constituency vote	Constituency seats	Share of regional vote	Regional seats	Total seats
Labour	32%	37	29%	9	46
SNP	33%	21	31%	26	47
Conservative	17%	4	14%	13	17
Liberal Democratic	16%	11	11%	5	16
Green	0.1%	0	4%	2	2
Others	2.1%	0	11%	1	1
		73		56	129

Table 2.3 Elections to the Scottish Parliament of 2007

There are very important points to note here. Look at the way in which smaller parties get representation and the fact that no party has a majority in the Scottish Parliament.

Note carefully the wide range of different electoral systems used in the UK.

1.10 The Welsh Assembly elections

The Welsh system is virtually identical to the Scottish system. The simple plurality system is used in the 40 'ordinary' constituencies. A further 20 members are elected — using closed party lists — from the five regions, which are the same as European constituencies.

1.11 Elections to the Northern Ireland Assembly

A very different system was adopted in Northern Ireland to ensure that Roman Catholic voters were properly represented. It is a proportional representation system. It has not produced a majority government, but it does result in power sharing/coalition governments which have played a major part in the peace process. You can see how the number of seats reflects the percentage of votes.

Party	Share of the vote	Seats won
DUP	30.1%	36
SF	26.2%	28
SDLP	15.2%	16
UUP	14.9%	18
AP	5.2%	7
GP	1.7%	1
PUP	0.5%	1
Others	0.5%	1
Total		108

Table 2.4 The Northern Ireland Assembly elections of 2007

2 *The first-past-the-post system*

Given the results of the 2010 UK general election, how strong is the case for electoral reform?

The proper name for the system used in UK general elections is the simple plurality system. However, it is frequently called the first-past-the-post (FPTP) system. The UK is divided into 650 single-member constituencies, each sending one MP to Parliament. Regardless of how many candidates stand in a constituency, the candidate with the greatest number of votes is the winner, even if the majority of those who voted did not vote for the winner. Those who wish to stand as candidates must put down a deposit of £500 (£5,000 if standing for election as an MEP), which is returned if the candidate gets more than 5% of the votes cast. This is designed to stop too many candidates standing. There are very strict rules about how much money each candidate can spend. (See the Political Parties, Elections and Referendums Act of 2000.)

2.1 Advantages of first past the post

The merits of this system (designed in 1885 by the Conservatives and Liberals to ensure that radical parties would not win any seats) are as follows:

- It is simple to operate and understand.
- The results are easily understood.
- It tends to give the winning party a larger proportion of the total seats than its proportion of the votes. The largest party usually has a clear majority, which avoids the need for coalition governments, where two or more parties have to join together to form a government. Coalitions can involve a lot of negotiating and 'deals' before a government can be formed, or it can lead to a minority government.
- Each constituency gets an MP who has to look after the interests of that constituency and its inhabitants. There is a strong local link between the MP and his or her constituency.
- It usually produces a government with a majority (but look at 1974, 1992 and above all the 2010 elections).

2.2 Disadvantages of first past the post

- Too often a majority of the voters in a constituency vote against the winner. This could be seen as undemocratic. Representatives can get elected on tiny amounts of public support. In 2005, for example, George Galloway polled the votes of only 18.4% of his constituents and was elected. Only three MPs elected in 2005 secured the votes of more than 40% of their constituents.
- A government can represent only a minority of the voters. Labour won in 2005 with only 36% of the vote (on a 61% turnout).
- It is possible for the majority of the voters to vote for one party, while another party actually gets more seats and therefore wins the election. This happened in both 1951 and 1974.
- It can result in 'safe' seats — one party always winning the seat in a particular constituency. This is not good for democracy and can discourage voters from voting. MPs need to be accountable.
- A few voters changing their minds in a few marginal seats can change a government. For example, look at the figures for 1974.

- It can lead to a situation such as in Scotland in 1997, when nearly 20% of the electorate voted for a party (the Conservatives) and yet that party did not win a single seat in Parliament for that country.
- Voters only have one vote. What happens if they like the candidate for one party, but dislike most of the ideas that the candidate's party represents?
- Minor parties lose out. In the elections of 1983 and 1987 the Liberal Democrats got approximately 25% of the vote and approximately 3.5% of the seats. In 2010 the Liberal Democrats got 23% of the vote and 57 seats, while Labour got 29% of the vote and 258 seats.
- There can be a huge bias against a party because of the way its vote is distributed around the UK. The Conservatives suffered badly in this respect in 2001 and 2005.

Party	Share of the vote			Seats won		
	2001	**2005**	**2010**	**2001**	**2005**	**2010**
Labour	42%	36%	29%	413	355	258
Conservative	33%	33%	36%	166	197	306
Liberal Democratic	19%	23%	23%	52	62	57

Table 2.5 First past the post in practice: the UK election results of 2001, 2005 and 2010

2.3 Tactical voting

Another perceived failing of the first-past-the-post system is that it can lead to **tactical voting**. This occurs when voters in a constituency who happen to support party A realise that there is no chance of their favoured party winning, so they vote for party B in order to try to stop the candidate for party C winning. They dislike party C most, so they vote for a party they don't dislike as much, but don't really prefer, as the lesser of two evils. One of the reasons why both Labour and the Liberal Democrats did so well in 1997 and 2001 was tactical voting: many Liberal Democrats voted Labour in some seats to keep out the Conservatives, while in other constituencies Labour voters backed Liberal Democrats also to keep out the Conservatives. There is less evidence that tactical voting played such a strong role in 2005 and 2010, possibly as anti-Conservative feeling was less strong.

3 *Other electoral systems*

You need to have a reasonable working knowledge of other types of electoral system, particularly those in use in other nations of the EU. There are two broad types:
- proportional electoral systems
- **majoritarian** electoral systems

Tactical voting: the practice whereby a voter does not vote for his or her first preference party (which may not stand a chance of winning a seat), but votes for another party in order to keep out a third party that the voter particularly dislikes.

Is it 'undemocratic' to have tactical voting?

Majoritarian systems: electoral systems which require the winning candidate, at either local or national level, to receive more than 50% of the total vote.

3.1 Proportional systems

The main proportional systems are as follows:

The list system

This is used in EU countries such as Belgium and Spain. Quite simply it means that if a party gets 45% of the votes cast, it gets 45% of the seats in Parliament. The constituencies tend to be very large, with as many as 20 MPs being elected for each. It is mathematically very correct, but it is criticised for giving a lot of power to the parties themselves, which decide the candidates on their lists. Also it does not always produce MPs with a strong constituency link.

The single transferable vote (STV) system

Under this system a country is divided into multi-member constituencies: in Ireland, for example, they are county-sized, each returning several MPs to the country's parliament. Five is a common number. The voter has five votes in a five-member constituency, and lists his or her votes in order of preference. If a candidate gets more than 20% of first preference votes, he or she is elected. Once a candidate gets more than 20% of the votes cast, the remainder of his or her votes are transferred to the voters' second choices. To be elected, a candidate has to get a quota, and the quota is worked out by using the Droop formula:

$$\text{quota} = \frac{\text{total number of votes cast} + 1}{\text{number of seats in the constituency} + 1}$$

Parties tend to take a lot of care in selecting candidates under this system in order to give the electorate plenty of choice — for example, there are more women candidates. The constituency link is retained, the voter gets more choice and the number of seats won by parties tends to reflect the proportions of the vote they received nationally. Voters tend to vote for candidates and not parties, and it is in the interests of all parties to work hard at election time to educate the voters about the merits of their candidates. In some countries it produces a majority government; in others it does not. It is worth noting that there is no evidence that it produces political instability.

The additional member system (AMS)

This is the system adopted for elections to the Scottish Parliament, where voters have two votes, one for a constituency MP and one for a party.

3.2 Advantages of proportional representation

- It does not cause 'wasted' votes. A wasted vote can occur in a constituency when one party has a huge majority, usually over 20,000, and the wasted vote goes to the losing party. Wasted votes can account for as many as 70% of the total in some areas. Under **proportional representation** all votes count.
- There are fewer safe seats. In 1983 the Conservatives' vote dropped but they increased their seats. It took just 35,000 Conservative votes to produce one Conservative MP, while it took more than 300,000 Liberal Democratic voters to produce a Liberal Democratic MP. This does not happen under proportional representation.

Proportional representation: a system of voting which seeks to ensure that there is a direct mathematical relationship between the number of votes cast and the number of seats gained in an election.

The merits and demerits of proportional representation are very likely to feature as a question, so make sure you can present a balanced argument on this topic and back it up with accurate statistics.

- The government, which may be a coalition, represents a majority of the voters, and not a minority as under first past the post. The 17.5% of the electorate who voted Conservative in Scotland in 1997 did not have a single MP to represent their views in Parliament. Under proportional representation this would not happen.
- It tends to produce a more representative group of MPs, as in Ireland.
- It avoids the situation where a few marginal seats control the whole result.
- Parties whose vote is geographically scattered gain seats, whereas under first past the post the Conservatives in Scotland or in Sunderland cannot achieve representation.

3.3 Disadvantages of proportional representation

- The link between constituents and their MP may be lost.
- It might lead to constant coalition governments, with minority parties holding the balance between two much larger ones and thus wielding too much influence. It might be argued that this happened in the UK between 1976 and 1979, and again in 2010, under the first-past-the-post system. It is worth noting that some of the countries with the strongest economies and greatest stability in Europe use proportional representation.
- Accountability might be lost, with a small group in a coalition dictating policy, but the larger party having to take responsibility.
- The parties that make up a coalition might make secret 'deals' without the voters knowing.
- It can give too much power to the parties in deciding on their candidates.

3.4 Majoritarian systems

In addition to the UK's first-past-the-post system there are three other types of majoritarian system:

The two-ballot or second ballot system
This is mainly used in France. If a candidate wins more than 50% of the vote, he or she is elected. If no candidate gets more than half of the votes, the weaker candidates withdraw and there is a second election in which voters can reconsider their vote. The process continues until one candidate has more than 50% of the vote.

The alternative vote (AV) system
This is used in single-member constituencies, with voters listing candidates in order of preference. The candidate with the fewest first preferences is eliminated, and this process continues until one candidate has a majority.

Which system would you think is most suitable for the UK, and why?

The supplementary vote system
This was once supported by the Labour Party. In this system a voter has just two preferences. If no candidate gets 50% of the vote, all but the top two candidates are withdrawn and their second choices are distributed.

3.5 Advantages of majoritarian systems

- They keep the link between constituents and their MP.
- The winner (eventually) gets more than 50% of the vote.
- They tend to produce strong governments with majorities.
- They are easy to understand.
- There are no wasted votes.

3.6 Disadvantages of majoritarian systems

- They can encourage electoral pacts between parties to damage a third party, as parties tend to recommend that their voters put the other favoured party as second choice.
- They tend to favour centre parties.

In some cases a change of electoral system has been introduced in order to achieve a specific objective (as in the case of the Northern Ireland Assembly). Sometimes this is successful, but a look at what happened in New Zealand (switched from first past the post to proportional representation) and Italy (switched from proportional representation to first past the post) will show that changing your election system does not necessarily solve the problems you thought were caused by it. Election systems perhaps do not cause problems, but reflect them. The UK general election of 2010 put the whole issue of electoral reform back on the national agenda.

4 Referendums

4.1 The history of referendums in the UK

A referendum is a vote on a single issue: for example, whether or not the voter wishes the UK to stay in the EU. Until recent years there was no tradition of holding referendums in the UK. Other countries tend to have them when a major constitutional change is being considered, and the UK is moving in a similar direction.

You should know about the following referendums:

Northern Ireland, 1973
This referendum was called in the hope of finding a solution to the growing violence in Northern Ireland. Voters in Northern Ireland only were asked whether they wished Northern Ireland to remain in the UK. The result was very much in favour, but large sections of the population refused to vote in the referendum, so it had limited impact. The UK government did not agree to be bound by its findings.

Membership of the EU, 1975
Leading a government badly divided over membership of the EU (then known as the European Economic Community), Labour prime minister Harold Wilson called for the first major nationwide referendum on whether the UK should remain a member. The verdict was that it should. The referendum ended party disunity on the matter — for a while. Wilson was careful not to let the result be binding. It is unlikely that he (always a supporter of the EU) would have called

for the referendum if he had thought he might lose it. There was a strong feeling among opponents of the EU that the government propaganda machine was used unfairly to persuade people to vote to stay in. There was also criticism of the way the question was worded, with allegations that it was designed to produce an answer in favour of staying in the EU.

Devolution for Scotland and Wales, 1979

Partly as the price for keeping the Liberals' support for his minority Labour government, prime minister James Callaghan agreed to have a referendum in Scotland and Wales (the English were not consulted) on whether there should be devolution for Scotland and Wales. There was limited support in Wales for it, and although the majority of those who voted for it in Scotland were in favour, the government decided that as those who voted in favour were fewer than 40% of the total electorate, devolution had, in effect, been defeated. Even then the government had not agreed to be bound by the result. As a result, referendums became rather discredited in the eyes of the public. Again it was clear that the government would not have embarked on the referendum unless it had been fairly sure that devolution would not win.

Devolution for Scotland and Wales, 1997

Voters in Scotland were asked two questions. The first was whether they wanted a Scottish Parliament and the second was whether they wanted the Scottish Parliament to have tax-varying powers. On both issues they voted 'yes'. The Welsh were asked only one question about limited devolution. This time the government did agree to be bound by the results, and devolution has subsequently gone through. Here the government supported the measures, which had been in the Labour manifesto. But Tony Blair's government was anxious not to be seen as pushing through a huge constitutional change without consultation, just by using its large parliamentary majority. The fact that Labour dominated the Scottish Parliament initially might be noted. Note the very low turnout in Wales: 50.3%.

Northern Ireland, 1998

This had two purposes: first, to get support for the Northern Ireland peace process, and second, to get endorsement for devolved powers to Northern Ireland and end the direct rule of Northern Ireland from London. As many political leaders in Northern Ireland opposed the peace process, the referendum was seen as an appeal by the UK (and Irish) government, going over the heads of the politicians and paramilitary leaders directly to the people. With a high turnout and more than a two-thirds majority in favour, this put real pressure on the political leaders of Northern Ireland to accept the Good Friday Agreement.

The mayor of London, 1998

This referendum asked the people of London if they wanted an elected mayor with powers to deal with certain aspects of London, such as transport. The result was positive, but the turnout was very low.

Regional Assembly for the North East, 2004

The voters of the North East were asked whether they wanted devolved power and a regional assembly. They rejected the idea overwhelmingly, in spite of strong government backing for it, on a 48% turnout.

> Referendums have mainly been used to deal with major constitutional issues. Should they be used for more 'political' issues such as immigration?

There have been promises of referendums on the euro, the EU constitution and the Lisbon Treaty, but they have not materialised. David Cameron promised in 2009 that if he were elected, no more powers would go to the EU without a referendum. (He was vague when asked to define 'powers'.)

4.2 The case for referendums

To what extent are politicians only enthusiastic about referendums on issues on which they know they will win?

- They are highly democratic.
- They involve citizens in major issues that affect their whole lives.
- They encourage participation.
- They give government consent for a specific action.
- They can be used to overcome obstacles, as happened in Northern Ireland in 1998.
- They can end controversy on highly divisive issues, such as devolution (Scotland and Wales 1997) and membership of the EU (1975).

4.3 The case against referendums

- They go totally against the UK's traditional system of representative democracy, where elected representatives in Parliament make major decisions after debating all the relevant issues.
- Governments sometimes only hold them when they are sure they will win.
- The wording of the questions could be misleading, as was argued in the 1975 referendum.
- Some issues are highly complex, such as whether to join the euro. To make a good decision on a highly sophisticated topic requires a degree of expert knowledge, which many of the electorate will not possess. The electorate might also be too strongly influenced by a foreign-owned press which is hostile to the EU for its own purely commercial reasons.
- There is a risk that a decision, such as the reintroduction of capital punishment, might be forced on a government that thinks it is totally wrong and does not wish to implement it.
- There is a risk that majorities will use referendums to impose restrictions on minorities. A referendum on immigration and asylum, for example, could cause enormous problems.

This is a compulsory topic for AQA. For OCR is it one of the three optional topics in Section B of Paper 1, but it is worth remembering that information learned for this topic could be useful in either of the other two optional topics: UK elections and electoral systems. For Edexcel you are unlikely to get a direct question on voting behaviour, but good knowledge of it could be useful for other questions in Unit 1.

To do well in this topic you need to:

- ensure that you have a good knowledge of the theories and various trends and models of voting behaviour. Use a textbook published since 2008
- ensure you have a really good grasp of both the statistics of the 2010 election and the experts' reasons for the unusual outcome. This is the one topic where you need to be able to quote statistics to get the factual marks
- get a reasonable grasp of what happened and why in the elections from 1997 onwards, but don't get too carried away with too much history — it's the last two or three elections that really matter
- keep open minded and don't believe everything you read. Experts disagree strongly about voting behaviour and events have a habit of proving all of them wrong

Short questions

1 Explain what is meant by the 'rational choice model of voting behaviour'.
2 What were the key issues in the 2010 general election?
3 What is meant by 'tactical voting'?
4 How important is ethnicity in voting behaviour?

Essay questions

5 To what extent is social class still the most important factor in voting behaviour?
6 Discuss the view that the Conservatives failed to win the election of 2010 outright because of their policies.
7 'Campaigns are not important to electoral success; it is the party leadership that matters.' Discuss.
8 Discuss the view that the mass media play too important a role in voting behaviour.

1 *Models of voting behaviour*

One of the problems with models of voting behaviour is that it is easy to see where they are wrong, but not easy to suggest another good theoretical basis for voting behaviour. Try and get them in order of importance, and work out why you have them in that order.

Class: distinctions made between people based on factors such as parental background, job, education and lifestyle.

1.1 Social structures model

This model argues that social factors, such as **class**, age, gender and ethnicity play an important part in influencing voting behaviour. Which social class you belonged to was seen as the key factor in determining voting, with the middle class and above voting Conservative and the working class voting Labour. The flaw here was that the skilled working class tended to vote Conservative, and much of the Labour leadership came from the middle classes. However **class dealignment**, where voters do not see themselves as members of any specific class or identify with one, has been taking place. The statistics in Table 3.1 show this, but they also show that there is still evidence of class factors at work. Other 'social' factors also play a part, as Table 3.2 shows

Class dealignment: a decline in the correlation between social class and voting behaviour.

	AB			C1			C2			DE		
	1992	2005	2010	1992	2005	2010	1992	2005	2010	1992	2005	2010
Conservative	53	37	36	48	36	42	40	40	39	29	25	28
Labour	23	28	29	28	32	26	39	33	22	52	48	44
Lib Dem			28			26			24			15

Table 3.1 Social class and voting behaviour in the elections of 1992, 2005 and 2010 (%)

	Men 18–24	Women 18–24	Men 25–34	Women 25–34	Men 35–54	Women 35–54	Men 55+	Women 55+
Labour	36	33	23	37	28	32	27	30
Conservative	35	25	40	27	34	35	39	44
LibDem	23	36	22	25	25	26	18	19

Table 3.2 Gender and age and voting behaviour in the general election of 2010 (%)

Make sure you have up-to-date statistical knowledge of the 2010 election.

	Black and Asian voters		
	1992	2005	2010
Conservative	10	14	16
Labour	81	58	66

Table 3.3 Ethnicity and voting behaviour in the elections of 1992, 2005 and 2010 (%)

1.2 Party identification model

This model suggests that voters identify with a party at a young age and remain loyal to it in voting terms throughout their lives. The voter might in exceptional circumstances vote for another party. The reasons for the early identification with one party tends to be social and economic. However, this is seen very much as a declining factor in voting behavior. It influenced over 90% of voters in 1951 but well under 20% by 2010. This drop in class identification with a party is known as **party dealignment**. Better education, less thinking in class terms and a poor perception of parties are seen as the causes of this drop in automatic party support.

Party dealignment: a decline in the number of people who strongly identify with a particular political party.

Learn how to explain clearly these models of voting behaviour.

1.3 Rational choice model

This model of voting behaviour argues that voters make up their minds not because of the class they belong to, or their age or gender, but by exercising a rational and reasonable choice based on party records, policies offered in manifestos and voters' perception of party leaders. While it sounds plausible, evidence seems to indicate that voters are more influenced by what they perceive to be in their best economic interests (but don't always get it right!).

1.4 Dominant ideology model

The dominant **ideology** model argues that those dominant elites, who control the mass media, decide on the sort of questions that voters should ask and issues they should consider prior to voting, thus predetermining the outcome. For example, in 2001, the 'agenda' that was set by the dominant elite was 'Labour has done well since 1997 and deserves another term, doesn't it?' And in 2010 it was the 'Gordon has lost it, hasn't he?' message that was put forward. There is an element of a conspiracy theory about it, but the theory has validity.

Ideology:
a set of core beliefs, ideas or principles usually covering political, economic and social values. An example might be 'reduce the role of the state', and the policy which comes from that might be for a government to cut back its regulation of banks.

1.5 Voting context model

This model argues that voting behaviour is strongly influenced by the context or circumstances in which the election is held. For example, has there been a major crisis, such as the 'credit crunch', and are the voters looking for the right leader to sort it out? Is there a new party leader who is looking for endorsement? Are voters using the election to pass judgement on the current government's record? Has a government been in office for a long time and the voters are looking for a change? It can also apply to local and EU elections which voters often use to pass judgement on the national government, not considering local or EU issues at all.

2   *Trends in voting behaviour*

There could well be a question on trends in voting behaviour, as opposed to explanations of it. The main trends are identified below:

- Less committed party support. Party membership has declined; there are fewer active and committed members. The number of those who strongly identify with a political party and would vote for them regardless has also declined from about 80% in the 1950s to about 8% in 2010.
- Decreased turnout. The percentage of voters who actually vote in general elections went below 60% for the first time in 2001. It went back up to 65% in 2010. It has dropped particularly among the young and the core voters of the two main parties. Getting your core vote out and appealing to the younger voters is critical for success. Given that the older you are, the more likely you are to vote may explain why care of the elderly became an issue in the 2010 election.
- Abstention. There is some (inconclusive) evidence that more voters are deliberately abstaining. Reasons suggested range from a dislike of the electoral system, the safe seat issue, alienation over a specific issue such as the Iraq war, or part of a wider alienation from politics which the MPs' expenses scandal accelerated.

- Tactical voting. This has been growing as the electorate has become more sophisticated and parties have become cleverer in utilising it. The number of constituencies where tactical voting has played a significant role in the result is growing. In 2005, it is claimed that the results in over 30 seats were the result of tactical voting, and there was a large amount of information available in 2010 on how voters could make better use of their votes. In 2010 a Labour cabinet minister, Peter Hain, publicly advocated it to keep the Conservatives out. There is no evidence to indicate it was important in 2010.

- Protest voting. This is clearly growing. The rise of third parties such as UKIP which only really offer a single policy, as well as the effect of issues such as university tuition fees in some university constituencies and the Iraq/Afghan wars in strongly Muslim seats indicates this.

- Fluidity. The floating voter is now in the majority and is an important fact of political life. The two major parties can no longer rely on the support of loyal voters and they have to work exceptionally hard on their image, appeal, policies, and campaigns and press support.

- The internet and new technology. This has allowed online campaigning and blogs etc to flourish, but the jury is still out on their impact. It is suggested that vote swapping or tactical voting has been strongly influenced by the internet, but some of the most determined tactical voting campaigns failed. Evidence points to surprisingly few voters using it as a source of information for elections. Those who used it most for information were 18–24 year olds, and their turnout was the lowest. Expert conclusion is that internet use was 'marginal but not irrelevant' in its impact on the 2005 and 2010 elections.

- Third party/minor support. This is now a major trend. In 1970, there were only 12 MPs from 'minor' parties. In 2010, there were 85 MPs who were not Conservative or Labour, getting 35% of the vote. The Green Party won its first seat, and both UKIP and the BNP increased their share of the vote.

How important was the internet and other new technologies to the outcome of the 2010 election?

3 *Factors which play a part in voting behaviour*

You need to be able argue which of these were the most important, and why, basing your case on evidence from the elections of 2001 to 2010. Remember there is considerable disagreement among experts on this issue.

3.1 The influence of the campaigns

Both political and academic experts disagree about how many voters have not made up their minds before the start of the campaign, which usually lasts 3 weeks. Nor is there any agreement about the actual impact of a campaign on voting behavior. Some argue that Labour's campaign of 1992 in fact alienated voters because it was overconfident and 'triumphalist'. Others argue that its brilliantly slick and carefully managed campaign of 1997 was critical to its success, and showed Labour to be competent and efficient, in contrast to the Conservatives. On the other hand, some people argue that the campaign only added marginally to Labour's victory in 1997 — it was going to win anyway. In 2001, it was felt that a poor Conservative campaign helped Labour to win again, but was not a decisive factor. Extensive polling in 2005 indicated that while it may have affected turnout, the campaign had virtually no impact on voting

There is some evidence that the individual candidate could make a bigger difference in the 2010 election.

behaviour. Campaigns are becoming increasingly national in focus, although both parties targeted who they thought were likely supporters in key marginal seats. It is felt that a good new candidate who works hard in a campaign rarely makes more than 700 votes' difference in a constituency.

The 2010 campaign

Views vary on the importance of campaigns and the 2010 campaign is no exception. The polls issued in the weeks before the election date was finally announced matched up almost perfectly with the exit polls on 6 May and the final result. Arguably the campaign made no difference.

Labour's campaign was criticised because:
- It was felt that it did not stress the achievements of 'New' Labour.
- It failed to appeal to its core voters.
- It made too little contact with 'ordinary' people, and when it did in 'Bigotgate', it backfired badly (yet there was a swing to Labour in that seat).
- The image that Gordon Brown projected was unfortunate.
- Gordon Brown did not debate well on television.
- The party was clearly divided, both on policies and on its leadership.
- They were unable to put forward good reasons for not wanting a change in government, or why people should vote Labour.

The Conservative campaign was criticised because:
- It failed to capitalise on a weak economy, Gordon Brown's unpopularity, Labour's divisions, the fact that it had much more money than the other parties, a telegenic and popular leader and a good campaign in the marginals.
- The campaign in the marginals seemed to have little effect.
- There was no 'big theme', and no really clear messages on the economy, society or politics. Advocating spending cuts is not a good idea, however honest.
- The 'Big Society' theme of David Cameron frightened and confused voters.
- It had too 'presidential' a focus and did not capitalise on the anti-politics mood within the electorate.
- It did not offer a clear policy on immigration and asylum seekers, which was an issue that concerned many.
- There was no appeal to Scotland, the ethnic vote or the public sector voter. All have votes and clearly did not vote Conservative. Also they did not really appeal to the English/overtaxed/private sector voters who were prepared to seriously consider voting Conservative.
- The Conservatives lacked the killer instinct of Blair, Campbell and Gould of 1997.
- They made a mistake in agreeing to participate in the televised debates. The Conservatives were going to win without participating, and the debates allowed Nick Clegg to make a large impact.

Look carefully at individual parties' post mortems on their election campaigns.

The Liberal Democratic campaign was criticised because:
- They did not capitalise on the 'surge' after the first televised debate and 'Cleggmania'.
- Some policies were not popular, especially those on the EU , immigration and asylum seekers.
- It became too 'presidential' with the focus on the leader and not on the policies.

- It was too focused on what might happen in the event of a hung parliament and did not focus on what was good about Liberal Democrat policies and the failings of the other parties.

3.2 Regional factors

You can see the substantial differences in party support between regions. Table 3.4 shows the average change in percentage share of the vote since 2005.

Region	Conservative	Labour	Lib/Dem	Nationalists
London	+3.1	−2.8	+0.1	
South East	+4.8	−8.2	+0.1	
South West	+4.3	−7.6	+2.0	
East	+3.4	−10.3	+2.0	
E Midlands	+4.0	−9.3	+2.2	
W Midlands	+4.5	−8.1	+1.8	
Yorks and Humberside	+3.9	−10.0	+0.1	
North East	+4.0	−10.0	−0.1	
Wales	+4.4	−7.0	+1.5	−1.2
Scotland	+4.4	−7.0	−1.2	+2.1

Table 3.4 Average change in percentage share of the vote since 2005.

3.3 The role of the media

There is no agreement among experts about how much influence the media can have either on voting behavior or in what areas. However, a number of pieces of evidence are relevant:

- Most people in the UK read a newspaper. In 1992 the majority of newspapers supported the Conservatives and they won. In 1997, 2001 and 2005, the majority of newspapers supported Labour and they won. In 2010 the vast majority supported the Conservatives with unusual enthusiasm for months before the election and during the campaign. Even the usually loyal *Guardian/ Observer* group left Labour and supported the Liberal Democrats. However, Labour did not suffer the landslide defeat the media predicted.
- In the late 1980s and early 1990s, the general tenor of the press was critical of Labour and the image presented was that Labour was still a radical and divided party. In the final week of the 1992 election campaign, the media switched attention away from health and education issues (which favoured Labour) to taxation, which favoured the Conservatives. In spite of the economy being in poor condition, the Conservatives won in 1992. Although the majority of the newspapers were critical of Labour before and during the 2010 campaign, there was no focus on any issue which would either seriously harm Labour or benefit the Conservatives. The saturation coverage of the televised debates, especially the first one, benefited the Liberal Democrats, harmed the Conservatives and had little impact on Labour.

Always remember
that newspapers
think they are much
more important to
voting behaviour than
they actually are..

- After the economic crisis of 1992, the media became increasingly hostile to the Conservatives, and were particularly critical of the government's competence. In the run-up to the 1997 election, the media focused on 'sleaze' and Europe, closely followed by education and health, and these were issues that showed the Conservative government in a poor light. The most worrying issue in 2010 was the state of the economy and the attempts by the Conservative press to denigrate Labour's management of the economy failed.

- It is also argued that what the media choose *not* to mention can be important. For example, in 1997 and 2005, the healthy state of the economy, with falling unemployment and inflation, and large increases in health and education spending, received little mention. Nor did the huge achievement of bringing about peace in Northern Ireland. Some of the more radical ideas of Labour, particularly on the constitution, also received little attention in the media. The media focus in the final stages of the 2005 campaign on the 'trust' issue and the Iraq war were felt to have played a large role in reducing the size of the Labour majority. In 2010 there was a tendency to focus on the character and personality of Gordon Brown, and ignore Labour policies.

- Experts argue that the way in which Labour was presented in 1997 as 'fresh and energetic' compared with the 'tired and divided' Conservatives was important. The media consistently emphasised that 'New' Labour had given up its old socialist policies. The focus of the media on negative aspects of all three of the major parties in 2005 was felt to have played a large part in the low turnout (61%) and the small swings (e.g. Conservatives +0.6%). Again in 2010, the negative focus on the media may well have kept turnout low (65%).

- Current expert thinking is that the media do play a key role in persuading core voters to vote (or not), play an important role in influencing what the public sees as the key issues in an election, and influence some voters to change sides (but no one knows how many).

- In 2010 the evidence would indicate that the impact of the media was limited, in spite of perhaps one of the most sustained attacks by the press on a sitting government, and one of the most savage personal attacks on a politician — Nick Clegg by the *Daily Mail* (who linked him to Nazism), the *Daily Express* and the whole of the Murdoch press, when they thought the Liberal Democrats might take Conservative votes and keep Labour in. It is possible that from the Conservative point of view, it was 'The *Sun* wot lost it'.

3.4 Leadership

Experts agree that the public's perception of leadership competence is increasingly a critical factor in explaining voting behaviour. Blair was seen in polls as much more competent than Hague as a possible leader, and won comfortably in 2001. Blair was seen as a bit more competent that Howard in 2005, and won, but with a reduced majority. The Murdoch press campaign against Brown, which started in 2009, had a primary focus on his poor leadership. Certainly the polls indicated that Gordon Brown's style of leadership was a factor in not voting for Labour in 2010, but also concerns about the inexperience and 'shallowness' of David Cameron was a factor in not voting Conservative.

3.5 Image

The image that a party presents for itself, via television and other forms of advertising, and the media chooses to reflect, can also be vital. In 1997 the image of 'New' Labour, fresh, united, having broken away from the 'Old' tax-and-spend Labour contrasted with a Conservative party divided over Europe, weakly led and disliked for its 'sleaze'. In 2010 there was polling evidence that the fresh and youthful image of both the Conservatives and Liberal Democrats was a factor in their support.

3.6 Ideology

Again a there is a great debate over ideology. Some argue that the more 'ideological' a party becomes, the more it appeals to its core voters and alienates the floating voters. Hague's move to the right in 2001 over issues like the EU and asylum and immigration brought out the core Conservative voters, but Blair won comfortably. The lack of ideological commitment on the part of the Conservative Party under Cameron could be seen as a key factor in the rise of UKIP. In 2010 David Cameron's obvious lack of ideology and his move to the centre 'Blairite' ground was important in gaining votes. However there were signs of ideology in his 'Big Society' theme, but they played little part in the campaign. Signs of traditional Labour ideology, in ring-fencing spending on education and healthcare, were there, but there was little that could be called socialist. The party with the most obvious amount of ideology was the Liberal Democrats and it probably had limited electoral impact.

> Really make an effort to identify party ideology as well as party policies in the manifestos.

3.7 Policies in manifestos

Manifesto **policies** are another subject for controversy. Few voters read them and public awareness of what is or is not in a manifesto depends largely on which parts the media choose to focus on. Given the current level of voters' mistrust in politicians, the evidence indicates that manifesto policies have little impact. The coalition government of 2010 will inevitably make it impossible for the current government to implement many of its manifesto commitments. A quick look at the Conservative and Liberal Democrat manifestos will explain why.

> Policy: a specific line or view taken on an issue. A government's policy on the NHS might be to increase funding for it.

3.8 Attitudes towards party competence in managing the economy and the country

Polls indicate that this is an important factor in voting behaviour. An important reason for Conservative victories up to 1992 was that they were seen as more competent to manage the country (and particularly the economy) than Labour. However, as a result of the major economic problems faced by the Conservatives after 1992, their internal divisions over Europe and their identification with 'sleaze', Labour was seen as more competent in 2001 and 2005. In 2005, 49% of voters felt that Labour was good at managing the economy, compared with 27% for the Conservatives. In 2010 the media campaign against Gordon Brown raised concerns about his competence in economic matters, in spite of his and Chancellor Darling's management of the crisis of 2008–10. However the polls in 2010 did not indicate much faith in the Conservative's possible management of the economy.

3.9 Issues

Yet again a subject for debate. There are examples where the party seen to be 'best' on what voters identify as the key issues (e.g. health and education in the case of Labour in 1992) still loses. Correct identification by a party of what voters see as the key issues can help, as was the case with Labour in 2001 and 2005. Given that there is now such consensus between the two main parties on issues like health, education and foreign policy, how well those issues are managed is of more importance than the issues themselves.

3.10 Personal prosperity

US presidential candidate Clinton argued in 1992 that they key factor in elections was: 'It's the economy stupid'. It is the voters' guess as to which party might give them greater personal prosperity, be it in providing childcare or ensuring their bonus, that is a key motivator. The desire for change, so strong in 1997 and in 2010, is the other motivator, but both are not often directly articulated by the voters.

3.11 Electoral system

Inevitably the first-past-the-post system is bound to play a role, but again no one knows how much. How many potential Liberal Democrat voters are put off by the system? How many potential Conservative voters might be put off if they live in a safe Labour seat? How much tactical voting does it lead to? How many voters like a candidate but dislike their party? The prevailing view is that the current system helps Labour and harms the Conservatives and Liberal Democrats.

3.12 Opinion polls

Analysts disagree about how much influence opinion polls have on elections. In France they are banned in the weeks before an election because it is felt they have a damaging influence on voting behaviour. Some argue that polls might keep potential supporters at home because, if they see the party they support ahead in the polls, they think there is no need for them to vote. In contrast, some voters might be so dispirited at seeing their party 'losing', they also stay at home. Others argue that polls can create a bandwagon effect, with some voters seeing one party ahead and voting for it in order to be on the winning side.

The polls on the whole predicted incorrectly in 1992, but the polling organisations subsequently made changes in their methods of consulting people, and have been accurate since then. Exit polls, taken from voters after they have voted, are seen as much more reliable than polls taken before the election. In 2010 the polls overall prior to the election campaign predicted the outcome very accurately.

Remember that a significant percentage (around 16%) of voters in 2010 had not decided how to vote a week before polling day.

4 Why has the electorate become more volatile?

Most of these points have been made before, but in a different context:

- There is much less party identification and lifelong commitment to a particular party. It is simply no longer seen as the 'done thing' to stick with one party regardless.

- Social and economic changes have led to the blurring of class boundaries and the growth of a 'middle' class which all parties target now.
- With a reduced turnout caused by core voters' abstention and a reluctance of the young to vote, it is very difficult to predict.
- Tactical voting has been on the increase. A growing sophistication among voters has led to committed supporters of parties voting for alternatives when they see no chance of their own party winning a seat.
- Third or minor parties or 'protest' parties are now seen to have a real chance of success. Look at the rapid growth of the Liberal Democrats to 2005 as well as the success of George Galloway's Respect party in 2005. In 2010 the number voting for parties such as the BNP and UKIP grew.
- With the lack of any clear-cut ideological division between the parties or any major policy differences either, it is hardly surprising that voters switch easily between them.

5 *Past general elections*

In the exams, you will be expected to have a reasonable knowledge of the previous three general elections, unless, like 1974, there are two in one year.

5.1 The 2001 general election

Possible reasons for Labour's victory

- Opinion polls had consistently predicted victory since 1997 and Labour was expected to win. This may have deterred possible Conservative voters from turning out to vote.
- Tony Blair had avoided giving any sign that the 'Old' Labour policies of 'tax and spend' would reappear.
- Labour conducted a good campaign and the Conservatives a poor one. The Conservatives might have chosen the wrong agenda (e.g. the euro and asylum seekers). The press was invariably hostile to, and critical of, the Conservative campaign. Conservative organisation during the campaign was also poor, and the press highlighted this. The potential Labour 'disasters' during the campaign, such as John Prescott's infamous punch at a protestor who had thrown an egg and the attacks on Tony Blair for health service failings, generally received gentle treatment from the media. Does this suggest good spin-doctoring? The Liberal Democrats improved their position considerably during the campaign, going from about 12% to 19%, which damaged the Conservatives.
- Radio and television are expected to remain impartial, but some critics argue that New Labour's spin-doctors were so good at manipulating them that Labour received highly favourable treatment of such disasters as the Prescott punch. Newspapers were overwhelmingly supportive of Labour — the Murdoch press in particular. Again there is debate among experts about the extent of media influence. The present consensus is that it was important to Labour's victory, but no one is sure exactly how important.
- Labour chose to debate and focus on the issues that were most important to the electorate. Polls indicate that voters saw health and education as the two most important issues and Labour ranked them first and third in the

degree of emphasis it gave them in the manifesto and the campaign. The Conservatives ranked them fourth and fifth, and focused the bulk of their campaign on Europe, which the public ranked only tenth. Commentators saw this as a serious error of judgement on the part of Conservative leader William Hague and a key reason why he resigned after losing the election.

- Some commentators saw management of the economy as critical to Labour's victory. Gordon Brown was seen as a 'safe pair of hands' by the affluent voters in London and the southeast who swung to Labour in 1997 and stayed loyal in 2001. Some commentators have reservations about this view, arguing that the Conservatives stayed in power in 1992 even though the economy was in a bad way, and lost power in 1997 at a time when the economy was exceptionally healthy. Some argue that the media chose not to emphasise Ken Clarke's economic success of 1992–97 during the 1997 campaign, but kept the focus on the 'Black Wednesday' disaster of 1992. It might be argued that voters did not see the economy as an 'issue' in 2001. They felt comfortable with Gordon Brown and seemed aware that inflation, interest rates and unemployment were well down on 1997.

- Tony Blair managed to adapt his policies to keep the core Labour voters while continuing to appeal to 'middle England'. The Conservatives and Liberal Democrats made no impact on Labour's traditional support. New Labour had clearly captured the centre ground of British politics. As one commentator put it, 'Blair has become the least bad choice of middle England'.

- Labour benefited hugely from the structure of the electoral system. Labour's vote was geographically concentrated in such a way as to gain maximum benefit from the first-past-the-post system. It is clear why Labour stopped talking about electoral reform! The electoral system also damaged the Conservatives quite significantly.

- Both the public and the media felt it was appropriate to 'give Labour another chance'. The electorate's main concern was to get better public services, and the voters felt that Labour was more likely to deliver on these matters. Certainly the Labour manifesto and campaign had greater focus on public services.

- The Liberal Democrats took even more seats, and these came from the Conservatives. The SNP vote was down in Scotland, which was beneficial to Labour as the Nationalists were its principal opponents there.

- The Labour vote held up well in traditional Labour areas, although fewer voters actually voted for it. In the north, 5 million people voted Labour while only 2.4 million voted Conservative. In the traditionally Conservative south, both Labour and the Conservatives received 6 million votes. Labour also continued to grow in traditionally Conservative suburbia.

- Labour lost a few core voters who may have stayed at home (or voted BNP in some cases), but it gained middle-class voters. The Conservatives still received 44% of the vote among the professional and managerial classes compared to Labour's 37%, but Labour got over 50% of the vote in all other classes. Labour had become much more socially inclusive than the Conservatives.

- Labour benefited from the agenda that the media had set for the election. The basic question posed to the public was 'Is Labour fit for another term?' and the recommended answer was very much 'yes'. The way in which the Conservatives were portrayed, even by radio and television that were supposed to be impartial, was that they were not fit to govern.

- Labour captured the public mood much better than the Conservatives did. The public wished to be led from the left of centre (but not too far left). Conservative promises to reduce taxation, which many felt would lead to a reduction in the quality of public services, simply were not liked by the electorate. It is worth noting that the Liberal Democrats, pledging to increase taxes to fund better public services, did well in former Conservative seats. The Conservatives simply failed to grasp what the electorate felt.

5.2 The 2005 general election

Why the Conservatives did not win

- The polls were always hostile and the 'bandwagon' effect was at work.
- The electoral system was biased against the Conservatives.
- There was no clear divide between the Conservatives and Labour over policy.
- Tax was not the issue they hoped it would be in the election and they supported the war in Iraq, which was a vote loser.
- Their focus on asylum and immigration only had real appeal to their core voters, or those who went off and voted UKIP and BNP. Asylum and immigration also made them look like a single-issue party, and that issue was not seen by the electorate as significant at the time.
- The media gave little support. Michael Howard was not seen as a good leader and as a likely prime minister.
- The party image was still poor and voters still had the Thatcher/Major years in mind. They failed to win over AB voters, and their support dropped again. They also did not appeal to ethnic voters.
- Their slogan of 'vote Blair and get Brown' backfired badly — that was what quite a lot of people wanted.

Why Labour won again

- The polls were always favourable and the bandwagon effect was clearly there.
- They took great care never to appear extreme. They kept the debate and campaign non-ideological.
- People on the whole liked what Labour had done and were going to do. Blair's unprecedented offer to stand down as prime minister was vital. Their vote among women, so important in 1997, stayed up.
- The electoral system really helped them, and they did not mention reforming it.
- They were more convincing on major issues such as health, education, pensions and crime. Labour very much retained the centre ground and controlled the agenda.
- Their party image was good: the Liberal Democrats were seen as disorganised and the Conservatives as limited. Liberal Democrat leader Charles Kennedy failed to provide enough of a real alternative to attract the disaffected Labour voters. The impression was that the Conservatives did not offer a real alternative in terms of leadership or policies.
- Labour's media support remained loyal and even the supposedly neutral television and radio did not focus on what the public might perceive as their weaknesses.
- Few of the electorate seemed to want change (in contrast with the 1997 and 2010 elections).

Why Labour had a reduced majority

- There was a low turnout; many of Labour's old core voters stayed away, again.
- The public disliked the Iraq war — no 'weapons of mass destruction' had been found. The ethnic vote dropped — the Iraq war played a part in this.
- There were doubts about the quality of Blair's leadership. Many forgot the achievements of the Blair government, such economic stability and peace in Northern Ireland, and simply did not trust him.
- There was a wish to punish Blair, but still keep the Tories out.
- The media attitude was not nearly as supportive as in 1997 and 2001, but had not switched enthusiastically to the Conservatives.
- The arrival of university tuition fees were of concern in some constituencies.
- Some felt need for change.

Other factors affecting the overall results

- There was a substantial growth in postal votes.
- The polls were virtually unchanged during the campaign — they always predicted a Labour victory.
- The Conservatives gained some ground from the Liberal Democrats, a different sort of protest vote.
- There were lots of odd and unexplained local and regional differences, even in neighbouring constituencies.
- Some may have felt need for a change, or they may have been angry with Blair over Bush and the Iraq war.

5.3 The 2010 general election

We will have to wait until 2011 to get the expert views on the reasons for the outcomes of the 2010 election, in which it could be argued that no party 'won'. Below are some of the factors which influenced voting behaviour in the 2010 election.

Why the Conservatives did not win an outright majority

- They sent out mixed messages to the electorate. Cameron presented a tolerant 'luvvy' image at times, while the Conservative right wing sent out a very different message.
- There were no simple, clear policies laid out which mattered to the voters and which voters could identify with. Voters quite liked Cameron, but did not think a lot of his party.
- They needed a massive swing to get a majority, a larger one than any party had acheived for many decades.
- They avoided asylum and immigration as an issue, one which clearly was of importance to many electors, but they talked too much about spending cuts, not a topic that appeals to many voters. The 'Big Society' idea was a flop, few voters could grasp it.
- Cameron simply did not appeal to the younger voter enough, or make a good enough impression in the vital suburban seats.
- They were complacent, having such a clear lead in the polls. However, simply not being led by Gordon Brown was not a strong enough attraction.
- They could not give enough convincing reasons why there should be a change of government. Cameron and his campaign failed to capitalise on the anti-Brown/Labour sentiments in the country.

- Cameron did not perform particularly well in the televised debates. Appearing on them was a major mistake as it led to 'Cleggmania' which probably cost the Conservatives votes.
- UKIP took some of the Conservative votes.
- The UK is too much of a centre/left nation to trust the Conservatives with power.

Why the Liberal Democrats did not do well

- Their policies had limited appeal.
- It would have been a great deal worse if Clegg had not put on such a good television performance.
- The electorate tended to see the choice as one between Brown and Cameron. The electorate was simply not prepared to see the Liberal Democrats as an alternative to Labour.
- 'Cleggmania' was anti-Labour plus anti-Conservative, but it was not pro-Liberal Democrat 'mania'.
- There was little liking for many of the Liberal Democrat policies, especially those on electoral reform, the EU and asylum and immigration. The idea of an amnesty for asylum seekers appalled many.

Why Labour did not win

- Labour failed to deal with issues such as poverty and failed to get its core vote out.
- Brown had a bad image as prime minister and there had been a sustained media campaign against him. 'Bigotgate' did not help, especially with the enormous coverage it was given in the media.
- The recession inevitably led to an anti-government swing.
- There was a real lack of difference between the two major parties, so those just wanting a change found it easy to swing to the Conservatives.
- There was no focus on what had been Labour's successes, such as peace in Northern Ireland, the huge improvements in health and education, or the constitutional changes such as the Human Rights Act and devolution.
- Labour's working-class support dropped and it failed to convince the electorate that it was the party of 'fairness'. They did not offer a clear vision or a strategy for what the voters might see as 'success'.

No one really seemed to like any of the major parties, yet independent candidates still did badly, such as Esther Rantzen in Luton. The expenses scandal had a variable impact, some of the worst offenders who did not step down were re-elected, and were even made ministers, while others who had emerged with great credit, lost their seats. There were very erratic swings, ranging from the 14% swing from Labour to Conservative in Cannock, to a swing to Labour in Rochdale, the home of 'Bigotgate'. There was plenty of evidence that individual candidates mattered more than had been the case in the past, as Labour holding Birmingham Edgbaston showed. It is not an easy election to draw any simple conclusions about voting behaviour from.

4 Political parties

This is one of the most important (and probably one of the most straightforward) of all topics. There is going to be a question on them, and for OCR there will be a compulsory question, so you had better get it learned. All the boards require knowledge of current party policies and ideologies, and the roles parties play in contemporary politics (note the word 'contemporary'), plus some idea of how they are organised.

To do well in this topic you need to:
- be very up to date with developments in the two major parties, and have a good idea of what is happening with the minor parties
- have a good working knowledge of the policies/ideologies of the parties in the elections of 2005 and 2010
- be very aware of what is happening to political parties in the era of coalition government

Short questions

1 What are the functions of political parties?
2 What is the role of party conferences?
3 How do the Conservative and Labour parties choose their leaders?
4 Explain what is meant by Thatcherism.

Essay questions

5 Discuss the importance of political parties.
6 To what extent are there differences in both ideology and policy between the Labour and Conservative parties?
7 To what extent are UK political parties democratic organisations?
8 To what extent was 'New' Labour different from 'Old' Labour?

1 The function and roles of parties

Political parties provide many vital functions in the UK democratic process. This is surprising considering that they are not popular organisations and they now attract few members and limited finance.

The most important functions of political parties are:
- to provide the government and the opposition parties in Parliament, regional parliaments/assemblies, and local councils
- to enable the government of the day to get its legislation passed by Parliament
- to recruit, train and promote politicians
- to offer voters a choice at election time, at national, local and European level
- to enable individuals to participate effectively in the political process — and to influence the decisions that affect their lives
- to enable the views of the public to be represented in parliaments or councils
- to link the governments in London, Edinburgh, Belfast or Cardiff with the individual in the localities

- to enable popular wishes to be transformed into policy or law
- to provide coherence to the whole political process
- to educate and inform the electorate about issues
- to be the means through which the voters can make politicians accountable: they are vital for democratic controls
- to be the means of communication between voter and government, both upwards and downwards

> Really focus on how vital parties are to the democratic process.

In summary, political parties are the means by which politics can be made to work in a democratic society. Without parties, mass democracy would be unworkable, as there is no way in which every individual can participate directly in all the decision-making processes of a democratic society. They may be unpopular organisations, but they are essential.

2 *The Conservative Party, its origins and development*

The modern Conservative Party dates from the 1830s, when Robert Peel persuaded the old Tory Party to adopt the name of 'Conservative' together with new policies and important organisational changes. Before then, the Tory Party had opposed any change at all and just represented the aristocracy. Peel also persuaded it to broaden its membership to include more than just aristocrats and landed gentry, and to appeal to the growing middle class — Peel himself was the son of a successful manufacturer.

In the course of the nineteenth century, the Conservative Party went through periods of 'conservatism', when it opposed the more radical Liberals and their desire for change, but there were several periods in the nineteenth century when the Conservative Party put major political, social and economic change through Parliament. In 1867 it was a Conservative government that gave the urban working class the right to vote. In the 1870s it was another Conservative government that started a programme of radical social reform which improved working and living conditions for the working class.

By 1900 the Conservative Party had a record of being flexible and adaptable with its policies, and being capable of radical changes.

2.1 The core beliefs/ideology of traditional conservatism

> Conservatism: an ideology that aims to keep what is best in society and opposes radical change. It can be a more flexible ideology (and more difficult to define) than either liberalism or socialism, as Conservatives can embrace radical change, such as entry into the EU.

The **Conservatives** has gone through periods of being 'ideological' in opposing change and standing for the great institutions of the monarchy, the Church of England, the House of Lords and the Empire. Its ideology can be seen as:

- traditionalist
- conservative
- elitist
- authoritarian
- nationalistic
- hostile to big government and big spending on welfare spending/education

Be prepared to explain the difference between policy and ideology.

In its less ideological periods it was:

- pragmatic and adaptable (perhaps in order to win elections!)
- willing to accept the inevitable — whether in giving the vote for all or in nationalisation of industries
- prepared to change institutions in the interests of social harmony

2.2 The modern Conservative Party

In the course of the twentieth century the Conservative Party retained its record for adapting to change. One of the first industries to be nationalised in the 1920s, electricity, was nationalised by the Conservatives. However, it was also the same Conservative government that broke the General Strike in 1926 and penalised the trade unions involved.

Consensus: broad agreement within a group. For example, there was broad agreement (consensus) among all political parties in the 1950s and 1960s that the National Health Service should remain and be fully funded.

Between 1945 and 1951 the Conservative Party opposed many of the welfare reforms and the nationalisation programme of Attlee's government, but realised that if they wished to be elected, they had to accept them, and that acceptance was key to their winning the election of 1951 and staying in power until 1964. That period was known as one of '**consensus**' politics, as there was little visible difference between the Conservative and Labour parties in terms of ideology or policy. In office from 1970 to 1974, Heath took the UK into the EU (or the EEC as it was then known) but came into major conflict with the trade unions, which led to the collapse of his government and defeat in the two elections of 1974.

2.3 Thatcherism

Margaret Thatcher (leader from 1975 to 1990) had a remarkable impact on the Conservative Party and took it in a very different direction. She had a clear ideology, and many of her policies were based on that set of beliefs, including the desire to:

- reduce the role of government — to have a smaller state
- give the individual more freedom
- allow market forces to influence the economy, and not to have the economy run by the government
- pursue deregulation, so that the state did not regulate everything — such as banks
- end state ownership of industries, such as the railways and the electricity industry
- end monopolies and encourage competition
- reduce the power of trade unions and organised labour
- reduce the welfare state, expecting the individual to look after themselves more — ending the 'nanny state', with its high costs and taxes
- reduce taxation

To what extent did Thatcher 'reinvent' conservatism?

Most of her policies were based on these beliefs. Massive privatisation took place, as did deregulation, and union power was radically reduced. Taxation was lowered. Many of her policies were continued by her successor John Major between 1990 and 1997.

2.4 The Conservative Party 1997–2005

During this period the Conservative Party was led in turn by William Hague, Iain Duncan Smith and Michael Howard.

You need a reasonable knowledge of William Hague's changes to the party structure, as well as to the changes in party policy between 1997 and 2005. The main changes to the party introduced by William Hague are as follows:

- Ordinary party members were allowed to vote for the leader. This happened in the selection of the successors to William Hague, Iain Duncan Smith and Michael Howard. Conservative MPs narrowed down the candidates to two, and party members then chose one to lead them. Since the 1960s it had been only Conservative MPs who could vote for their leader.
- A written party constitution was introduced. Until then the Conservative Party had managed without one. Leaders preferred it this way, as it enabled them to make the rules, which made them more powerful within the party.
- A national membership scheme was introduced to increase party membership and income. There were concerns that membership was falling and becoming increasingly elderly. There was a real shortage of party activists who would help at elections.
- There was greater involvement by party members in policy making through the Policy Forum. In the past, although there had been some scope for members to give their views on policy at conference and through their MPs, there was no formal way of doing this.

These changes, proposed in 1998 in a document called *The Fresh Future*, were approved in a vote of party members by 96% of those who took part (there was a 33% turnout). This consultation and more democratic approach continued with a referendum on Conservative policy on the euro. A majority of 84% of party members backed William Hague's policy of opposing it (on a 60% turnout).

The easiest way to see Conservative policies for yourself, and not through the eyes of a possibly biased journalist, is to look at the party's own website. The most important areas to consider are:

- taxation
- public spending
- defence, especially the idea of a 'European' force
- healthcare
- the European Union, the euro and the European Constitution in particular
- the role of government
- education
- law and order and policing issues
- attitudes to immigration and asylum seekers

Some commentators argue that William Hague moved the party much more to the right, as did his short-lived successors, Iain Duncan Smith and Michael Howard.

Manifestos: a party maifesto is a list of policies that a party promises to carry out if it wins the election, such as cutting taxation. All major parties publish a manifesto during an election campaign.

What were the main differences between the Labour and Conservative manifestos in 2005?

2.5 Key points in the 2005 Conservative manifesto

The main policy points in the 2005 Conservative manifesto were:
- cutting taxes
- more controls over immigration and fewer asylum seekers
- better discipline in schools
- cutting fees for students at university
- more police
- cleaner hospitals
- more accountability

Commentators felt that the Conservative manifesto did not offer a radical alternative to what the Labour Party was offering. There were no fundamental differences on most major issues. The biggest difference between the two parties lay in their attitudes to the EU, but even the Conservatives did not wish to leave it, and made virtually no mention of it in their manifesto or campaign.

2.6 The Conservative Party under David Cameron

Michael Howard resigned after the Conservatives' third election defeat in a row in 2005, and was replaced by David Cameron, who campaigned on the need for change. Cameron had been an MP since 2001, having come from a background of working in the media business and as a special adviser to ministers. Like Tony Blair, he had been in the shadow cabinet but had never held any ministerial office.

As leader of the opposition from 2005 to 2010, Cameron:
- was anxious to end the Conservatives' 'nasty party' image
- moved into the centre ground of politics taken over by Blair
- pushed childcare and the disadvantaged, plus work/life balance
- showed concern about the environment
- wished to reduce poverty
- wished to show more tolerance towards homosexuals
- accepted Labour's tax rises
- showed firmness towards Conservative MPs over expenses
- continued to demonstrate Euroscepticism, and allied Conservative MEPs with the far right in the European Parliament
- broadly supported Labour's management of the economy after the 2008 financial crisis
- strongly criticised Labour's deficit financing
- presented himself as a 'moderniser' and socially 'liberal', yet many saw him as very 'Thatcherite'
- was much more 'media savvy' then his predecessors, very much a student of the Blair/Mandelson/Gould school of 'spin' — he read polling evidence and acted on it
- was non-ideological

2.7 The 2010 Conservative campaign and manifesto

It is always difficult for a Conservative leader to create an election campaign and manifesto, as there is a strong section in the party which is 'right-wing',

very hostile to the EU, likely to vote for UKIP, strongly authoritarian and anti-immigration/asylum seekers. However, the leader also has to appeal to the floating 'centre' voter, who tends not to like extremism of any type.

What evidence was there of ideology?
- The centre/left focus, with a commitment to the NHS and education spending.
- The 'power to the people' idea.
- The 'Big Society' theme.
- The retention of traditionalist opposition to constitutional change and support for the Afghanistan military campaign, a strong stance on defence and anti-EU/federal ideas.

Generally there were few strongly advocated policies — the focus of the campaign was criticism of Brown and his management of the economy and social affairs. The Conservatives promised to:
- manage the economy successfully; reduce the deficit; cut tax, waste and spending; achieve greater deregulation
- restrict immigration and adopt a less tolerant approach to asylum seekers
- replace the Human Rights Act
- remain strong on defence, replace Trident, be supportive of the Afghan war
- accept the broad principles behind the EU but remain hostile to Lisbon, the euro and the transfer of any further powers to Brussels
- set schools and colleges free from state control and bring in tougher exams
- give strong support to, and remain committed to, the NHS
- be very 'pro-family', with some fairly generalised policies here
- be 'pro' the environment, but again without being very specific in terms of policy

There was little mention of culture, the arts, devolution or any major constitutional issues.

3 The Labour Party, its origins and development

The Labour Party was created in the early twentieth century, mainly by the trade unions, which provided the money and the voters, and by middle-class intellectuals, who added much in the way of a **socialist** ideology and organisational skills.

Although a Labour government was in office in the 1920s and 1930s, it never had a majority and therefore was unable to get through much of the 'socialist' legislation it wanted. Labour's first majority government took office between 1945 and 1951 — a period marked by the creation of the welfare state and the National Health Service, and a major programme of nationalising strategic industries. The country recovered well after a devastating war, and by the time Labour left office the government had attained full employment, achieved a balance of international payments and created a welfare state.

During the period 1951–79, when the Labour Party was in office it tended to have very similar policies to the Conservatives. On the main areas, such as the role of the government in managing the economy, foreign policy, and even public spending and taxation, there was no real disagreement between the two

Were there major differences in policy and ideology between Labour and the Conservatives in 2010?

Socialism: a political (and economic) ideology based on the state or the community owning the main means of production (e.g. steel factories), distribution (transport) and exchange (banks, etc). The welfare of the individual is less important than the welfare of the community as a whole.

parties. It is worth noting that Labour was split on entry into the EU (then the EEC) in 1972, and that the Conservatives (also badly split) only passed the Act to join the EU with the support of Labour MPs. The Conservatives who supported the EU returned the favour in 1975, when many Conservative MPs supported the Labour government in the referendum campaign to stay in the EU, even appearing on the same platform as Labour ministers.

3.1 The core ideology of 'Old' Labour

It was a socialist (not communist) middle way between conservatism and communism or anarchy. The main ideas were:
* optimism about humanity
* a belief that the community was as important as the individual
* a belief that the main industries of a nation should be owned by the state
* strong opposition to capitalism and the exploitation of people that went with it
* a class-based approach, favouring the working class over the others
* a strong belief in equality for all, even at the expense of liberty
* that the state should control the economy for the benefit of all
* that there should be a 'cradle-to-grave' welfare state

The sort of policies put forward as a result would be high taxation of the rich and the abolition of private education and healthcare, in order to get equality.

However, by the 1970s, in the light of experience and events, many Labour politicians (for example, Tony Crosland) began to see the need to modify some of the core principles. They began to question the merits of nationalisation of industry, and instead to see the merits of reducing state control of the economy. They wanted to spend much more on education, in order to increase opportunity, and to increase the role of the private sector generally, while adopting progressive (but not too high) taxation to redistribute wealth.

It was the disagreement between 'Old' (socialist) Labour and those with more progressive ideas that led to the Labour Party splitting badly in the 1980s.

3.2 The modern Labour Party

In 1979 the Labour Party under James Callaghan lost the election to the Conservatives under Margaret Thatcher. The party then moved very firmly in a markedly socialist direction. Under the leadership of Michael Foot and Tony Benn, not only was power in the party pushed very much down to the grassroots, but policies became much more socialist. Many members and MPs, including key former ministers such as Roy Jenkins, left to form a new party, the Social Democratic Party (since merged with the Liberals to form the Liberal Democratic Party).

In its 1983 manifesto, the Labour Party advocated:
* leaving NATO
* leaving the EU
* abolishing private medicine and private education
* giving up the nuclear deterrent
* hugely increasing nationalisation of finance and industry
* considerably increasing taxation and public spending

> Make sure you know the difference between a communist, a socialist, and 'Old' and 'New' Labour.

Why do you think the policies put forward by Labour in 1983 were unpopular?

These left-wing ideas played an important part in Labour's massive defeat in the election of 1983, and the manifesto was nicknamed 'the longest suicide note in history'. The Liberals and Social Democrats between them obtained nearly as many votes as the Labour Party did. It was a humiliating defeat for the Labour Party, and its chances of ever returning to power were seen as very thin.

3.3 The leadership of Neil Kinnock and Tony Blair, 1983–97

As a result of the defeat in the elections of 1979, 1983, 1987 and 1992, the Labour Party was prepared to introduce changes in its policies and organisation in order to make it capable of winning elections and forming a government. It became very clear in the course of the 1980s that many UK voters broadly approved of what the Conservatives under Margaret Thatcher were doing, and that unless the Labour Party adapted and took on board some of her ideas, it would remain in opposition.

The main changes in Labour Party organisation and policy in this period were as follows:

- The role and power of the trade unions within the party was reduced. Margaret Thatcher's policy of reducing trade union influence was very popular with the public.
- The Labour Party's reliance on the trade unions for funding was also reduced. Money would have to be gained from other sources — by attracting individual rich donors and increasing ordinary membership.
- The leader's power over membership, candidate selection, party structure and policy making was increased. This would enable the party to adopt more moderate policies that would appeal to the 'middle ground' of electors, who had deserted the Labour Party very obviously in the 1983 election.
- The influence of radical socialist groups such as the Militant Tendency in the party was ended, and their hold over local government in areas such as London and Liverpool was destroyed. The damaging media portrayal of the work of party members such as Derek Hatton in Liverpool and Ken Livingstone in London was seen as having driven away traditional Labour voters.
- The party moved much further to the 'right' to win over middle-income and middle-class voters. With class realignment taking place on a very large scale, traditional working-class Labour voters were now a much smaller part of the electorate. If Labour advocated policies that only appealed to this decreasing proportion of the population, it would never regain power.
- The party abandoned its traditional 'tax and spend' policies. The public clearly liked Margaret Thatcher's reductions in direct taxation — particularly income tax — and would not vote for a Labour Party that advocated a serious increase in taxation.
- It accepted the popular privatisation programmes of the Conservatives. A very large number of potential Labour voters had bought shares in newly privatised industries such as gas and telecommunications. Also, many potential Labour voters had bought their former council houses.
- The party accepted the idea of devolution for Scotland, Northern Ireland and Wales, to which James Callaghan and 'Old' Labour had been very hostile.
- It accepted membership of the EU and NATO — in fact, it became enthusiastic about membership of both.

- It accepted the existence of private healthcare and private schools. Several major trade unions had actually negotiated agreements for their members with large employers, which included membership of private health schemes.

Note the key differences between 'Old' and 'New' Labour.

The party leadership referred to the changed party as 'New Labour' to make it clear that there was a real distance between it and the 'Old' Labour Party of 1983 which had proved so unpopular with the electorate. Many of the changes were the work of Neil Kinnock, the Labour leader until 1992, when the Labour Party narrowly lost the election of that year. The changes in the Labour Party are seen by many commentators as a remarkable achievement on his part, and one of his key aides in the process of 'modernising' the party was Tony Blair.

3.4 The Labour Party in government, 1997–2001

Tony Blair tried to achieve what he called his 'Third Way' between 'Old' Labour's socialism and the free-market ideas of Margaret Thatcher. The main areas to look at to see what 'New' Labour, stood for are:
- public spending and taxation
- health and education
- the management of the economy by Gordon Brown and the Bank of England
- the Social Chapter and the Human Rights Act
- devolution to Wales, Scotland and Northern Ireland, and the other constitutional changes such as Lords reform and Freedom of Information
- the Northern Ireland peace process
- the 'Welfare to Work' programme, benefits and pensions
- the euro, the 'ethical' foreign policy, Kosovo and the 'war on terrorism'

You should be able to work out for yourself how 'new' New Labour is, and how it might differ from 'Old' Labour.

3.5 The Labour Party manifesto, 2001

A detailed working knowledge of the 44-page, 28,000-word document is not required, but knowledge of the key points is, so that you can deal with questions on party policy and ideology, and also with questions on the general election of 2001. It is worth noting that the manifesto contained seven photographs of Tony Blair, and none of any other Labour politician.

The main points in the manifesto, entitled *Ambitions for Britain*, were:
- opposition to any increase in income tax
- support for the EU and the promise of a referendum on the euro
- more teachers, doctors and nurses, and a willingness to work with the private sector in both health and education to improve services — education was the 'number one priority'
- investment of £180 billion in road and rail improvements
- more police and a tougher stance on law and order
- extension of the 'Welfare to Work' programme — 'The benefits system will be restructured around work'
- a tougher line on asylum seekers
- minor constitutional changes to the House of Lords and a 'possible review' of proportional representation by 2003

Commentators did not feel that the manifesto was a radical document in any way, and it ought to be contrasted with the Conservative manifesto to see if there are any major differences in either ideology or policy. The main target appeared to be the middle-ground voter, who would be alienated by anything that looked too radical or 'socialist'.

There was a low turnout of voters — particularly among the social groups that traditionally support Labour (its core vote), as they felt that it contained too little which appealed to the poorer sections of the community, such as radically increased spending on benefits and pensions.

3.6 The Labour Party 2005 election manifesto

The key points to be aware of here are that the manifesto promised:
- no significant change to the earlier direction
- more choice and quality in public services — health and education
- more police
- support for the enterprise culture, with a continuation of the established economic and tax policies
- more immigration controls and restrictions for asylum seekers — and ID cards for all
- measures to appeal to the 'grey' vote as well as the 'green'
- more 'family-friendly' policies such as childcare and maternity/paternity leave provision

Most commentators felt there was no serious ideological division between the two major parties. Critics of Tony Blair within his own party accused him of abandoning 'Old' Labour principles and traditional core Labour voters.

3.7 Labour under Blair and Brown, 1997–2010

How much did Tony Blair change the Labour Party?

Judgements on these 13 years are bound to be subjective. These are the broad areas which you might look at in order to prepare for questions on 'New' Labour:
- Modernising the government and the party.
- Giving much more power within the party to the leader.
- Creating a 'catch-all party' which would appeal to the centre ground of politics.
- Broadly accepting Thatcherism, but trying to put a more human face on it.
- Being much more business-centred and favouring deregulation (modified in the light of the banking crisis of 2008!).
- Favouring further constitutional change.
- Bringing peace and stability to Northern Ireland.
- Intervening in Kosovo, Iraq and Afghanistan, and the so-called 'ethical' foreign policy.
- Maintaining a close relationship with US President George W. Bush.

Note also the following:
- What happened to public spending — especially on health and education.
- What happened to universities, in terms of fees, spending and expansion.
- Asylum and immigration issues.
- Economic management and the crisis of 2008.
- The EU — the euro and Lisbon.
- The 'war on terror' and the issue of civil liberties.

3.8 The 2010 Labour manifesto and campaign

Like his Conservative counterpart, the Labour leader does not have an easy task — although the old 'hard' left has largely gone, there are still some MPs and party activists who are strongly socialist in inclination and are unhappy with the ways in which Blair and Brown allowed market forces to dominate their economic thinking. Again, Labour leaders know that if they move too far to the 'left' they will alienate the middle-ground floating voters and resurrect fears of 'Old' Labour's 'tax and spend' policies.

The basic ideology reflected in the manifesto was to increase the role of the state in markets and in society.

The main policies outlined in the manifesto were:
- continuation of the Brown/Darling economic policies — no 'tax and spend', but sensible management of the deficit in a way which would not hit healthcare and education
- a job creation programme and improvements to the minimum wage
- broad support for the EU, but no adoption of the euro without a referendum
- an interventionist approach to police forces and schools which fail
- support for the NHS and education, with spending on both ring-fenced
- a family-orientated approach, with a focus on childcare
- a promise of constitutional reform

Few commentators felt there was much in the way of either ideological divide or policy differences between the two major parties. There was no great policy debate in the campaign. The Conservatives focused on the need for change and the 'Big Society' theme, while Labour emphasised their record and the need for experienced ministers to take the country through difficult times.

4 *The Liberal Democratic Party*

Exam questions often expect knowledge of the Liberal Democrats, but the boards don't specify it in their formal syllabus, so it is a good idea to have at least outline knowledge of them. However, in the light of the coalition government of 2010, more detailed knowledge is required.

The **Liberals** were a major force in the nineteenth and early twentieth centuries, and offered the alternative to the Conservatives until Labour came along.

Their core beliefs were:
- tolerance
- individual liberty
- limited government/checks and balances
- public welfare
- laissez-faire economics
- democracy
- pacifism

Liberalism: a political ideology that has as its main beliefs the preservation of the rights of the individual and giving all citizens the maximum freedom of choice. It focuses on the liberty of the individual and sees the purpose of the state as being to help the individual.

Liberal prime ministers played a key role in the early welfare state between 1906 and 1914. For various reasons the Liberal Party more or less died out after

1918 and it rarely had more than a handful of MPs until the 1970s. They tended to do well in by-elections and local elections. The party grew after 1979, largely through voter disillusionment with Labour, but also because of the rigour of Thatcherism; however the electoral system was very biased against them (see the 1983 election in particular). They benefited from a merger with the Social Democrats (a breakaway group of senior Labour figures) in 1981. In the 2005 election they won 23% of the votes cast and 62 seats.

4.1 Liberal Democratic policies since 1997

The Liberal Democrats have often been irritated by other parties pinching their policies! Their main policies are:

- constitutional reform
- devolution — to as low a level as possible
- the 'green' agenda — it was the first mainstream party to push this
- consumer rights
- strong support for the EU — the most 'federalist' of all parties
- strong support for welfare — committed to raising taxes to spend on health and education
- strong opposition to the Iraq war, and a very pacific foreign policy
- taxation of the very rich
- ending university fees

4.2 The 2010 Liberal Democratic manifesto

In some ways writing a manifesto has been easier for the Liberal Democratic Party leader than for the leaders of the two other main parties, since the party's policies were unlikely to be implemented. However, there is a very diverse membership, and members can be very radical. The leader does not have the degree of control over the manifesto which the Labour and Conservative leaders have.

Traditional Liberal ideology was:

- libertarian
- in favour of devolution of power
- tolerant
- European and internationalist
- pacifist

Contrast this with traditional Conservative ideology.

4.3 Key Liberal Democratic policies

In many respects the Liberal Democrats proved to be more radical and to the 'left' of the Labour Party, so a coalition with the Conservatives was surprising. Their key policies were:

- progressive taxation — much clearer on 'tax the rich' than Labour
- an immigration amnesty for some — much more tolerant than the other major parties
- a libertarian approach, for example abandoning plans for ID cards — an area in which they agreed with the Conservatives, but for different reasons
- a reduction in defence spending — not replacing Trident, for example
- enthusiasm for the EU — they would have a referendum on joining the euro
- very 'green', with a variety of specific polices in this area

How many of these
policies differ
from those of the
Conservatives?

- the introduction of proportional representation, votes at 16 and an elected House of Lords
- giving more power to local government, and general support for all types of devolution — directly elected police chiefs, for example

5 *Minority parties*

Where you live may influence what you see as a minor party (neither the SNP nor PC are minor parties in Scotland or Wales). You need to be aware of the impact they can have on politics. The parties that you should have at least some outline knowledge of are:

- The Greens — their policies are largely environmental, and fairly radical on other issues. They do have policies on major issues such as the economy and education.
- UKIP — mainly anti-EU, but also right wing and authoritarian, and focused on asylum and immigration.
- The BNP — racist, nationalist, anti-EU and authoritarian.
- Respect — opposed to war, privatisation and unemployment; standing for peace, publicly owned services and a decent future for all.
- The nationalist parties in Scotland and Wales — seeking more devolution and independence.
- The Northern Ireland parties (you will not be expected to grasp the differences here).

The minor parties can have an impact, in particular:

- They can have a real influence on local, national and EU elections — look at the last local and EU elections to see the effect that UKIP and the BNP made: they won seats.
- They can highlight and reflect a grievance or protest — look at the examples of John Taylor in Kidderminster and George Galloway in Bethnal Green and Bow in national elections.
- They can really put their 'cause' on the political map — look at the impact of the Greens.
- They can inflict electoral damage on other parties. Concerns that potential middle-class voters might defect to UKIP from the Conservatives and that working-class voters might defect from Labour to the BNP do influence party policy and tactics.
- They can have an impact on policy. There is evidence that Labour policy on issues such as housing, asylum and immigration is influenced by the BNP — remember Gordon Brown's promises on 'British jobs'? Cameron's open Euro-scepticism may well have had a UKIP influence.

5.1 The role and impact of minor parties in the 2010 election

The minor parties had much less impact than had been expected. One Green MP was elected in Brighton, while the BNP and UKIP attained little, although UKIP may have cost the Conservatives some votes.

One possible question is on the factors which influence ideology and policy of parties. Factors which might be considered are:

- events — for example, the banking crisis of 2008 might well alter views on state regulation
- electoral issues, such as the potential loss of votes to a minor party which has a popular policy
- leadership, where a strong, charismatic and able leader, such as Thatcher or Blair, can have a massive influence on policy and ideology
- social and economic change, such as the decline of the traditional working class or a massive rise in oil prices
- party membership, particularly if it is well organised and angry
- the media, which can be very influential, particularly in what they decide to focus on — look at the attitude of the bulk of the press towards the EU
- public opinion, which can be decisive on issues such as healthcare and taxation

6 *Party structure and organisation*

6.1 Party leaders

The Labour Party leader

Traditionally, the Labour leader was expected to behave in a more 'democratic' way than his or her Conservative counterpart, and to be much more obedient to the National Executive Committee (NEC), party conference, the trade unions and the parliamentary party. However, as a result of losing four elections in a row — in 1979, 1983, 1987 and 1992 — the party's desire to form a government overcame its traditional 'democratic' tendencies and enabled Neil Kinnock, John Smith and then Tony Blair to change the role of the Labour leader out of all recognition.

The Labour Party leader now pays far less attention to the unions, the NEC and conference. Kinnock and Blair succeeded in breaking the militant left, abandoned traditional socialist ideas and eliminated many areas of dissent within the party. The leader now has far more control over Labour MPs and local parties. Tony Blair and Gordon Brown were far more powerful figures within the party, in terms of making party policy and selecting parliamentary candidates, than any of their predecessors. They insisted on far greater discipline within the party, both inside and outside Parliament, and gained it.

Tony Blair and Gordon Brown were accused by critics both inside and outside the party of being 'control freaks'. But their defenders argue that the Labour Party would not have won three elections in a row, and achieved what it did, between 1997 and 2010 if it had not been disciplined and united. Blair and Brown insisted on playing a central role in drafting the Labour Party manifesto, and did so for all elections. Controlling the manifesto obviously gives the party leader control over the policy agenda of the government if it wins the election.

Tony Blair also imposed his own view of how general elections should be conducted. Labour campaigns are now run from a separate headquarters, removed from Labour Party head office. The winning election team, led by Peter Mandelson, Alastair Campbell and Bryan Gould in 1997, reported very

How much power should a leader have in a democratic party?

much to Blair, and not to the general secretary of the party as had been the case in the past.

Detailed knowledge of the structure of the party is not needed, but it would be a good idea to make sure you are aware of the role of the NEC, both in theory and in practice.

Conservative Party leader

In theory, the Conservative leader is much more powerful than the Labour leader, with the party traditionally practising a top-down model rather than the bottom-up model of Labour:

- The leader is free to choose both the cabinet and shadow cabinet (the Labour Party's shadow cabinet is elected).
- The leader has total control of the election manifesto, which in effect makes party policy.
- The leader appoints the party chairperson (the Labour equivalent is elected by conference): this gives the leader control of the party machine and the initial vetting of parliamentary candidates.
- The leader is not obliged to pay any attention to the wishes of conference, while in the Labour Party the conference is supposed to be 'sovereign'.
- The new constitution of the party actually states that 'the Leader shall determine the political direction of the party'.
- Hierarchy and strong leadership seem to be basic Conservative beliefs.

Traditionally, a Conservative leader found it easier to impose his or her personality and ideas on the party than a Labour leader. This was very much the case with Michael Howard, whose ideas and priorities dominated the Conservative campaign of 2005, and David Cameron in the campaign and manifesto of 2010. Cameron's decisiveness in dealing with Conservative MPs over the election expenses issue is a good example of his leadership ability.

Is a Conservative leader more powerful than a Labour leader?

6.2 The role of party conferences

All the major parties have annual conferences, which take place in the autumn of each year.

Labour Party conference

The Labour conference has several main functions. These are:

- to direct and control the party as a whole — in theory, the conference is the 'sovereign' body within the party
- to give ordinary members a chance to air their views, vote on issues and elect people to key positions in the party, such as membership of the NEC
- to enable ministers or shadow ministers to argue for new policies and test party opinion on them
- to make ministers debate and defend their policies if the party is in government
- to enable communication upwards and downwards within the party
- to allow ordinary members to meet the party's MPs and leaders

Overall the conference has lost power and influence in recent years, and the leadership has grown more powerful. In addition, very great care is now taken by the party leadership to control the agenda of conference, as well as those who may speak, so that the party does not debate divisive issues or appear

disunited. The media that attend will focus very closely on possible divisions within the party, and the electorate is thought to disapprove of disunited parties at election time.

The 2000 conference (when Labour was in government) was very influential in persuading the chancellor, Gordon Brown, to improve old age pensions, but the 2002 conference totally rejected the Private Finance Initiative — nevertheless the Labour government simply ignored the hostile vote and introduced it. Throughout the Blair and Brown governments conference was always very carefully managed and never posed a real threat to the leadership.

Conservative Party conference

Unlike the Labour conference, the Conservative Party conference has no formal role and is seen as an advisory body. However, it is seen as having an important role in:

- rallying party members
- obtaining open endorsement of policies already decided by the leadership
- testing out new ideas
- enhancing the status of ministers or shadow ministers
- giving an opportunity for communication between the party's leadership and its ordinary membership
- improving the media image of the party, demonstrating unity and support for the leader, and appealing to voters — it has very important public relations implications

Traditionally, conference is not seen as an important part of Conservative Party processes. The leadership might respond to strong pressure sensed at conference, but that is unusual. The Conservative Party is seen as a much more 'top-down' organisation than the supposedly more democratic Labour Party. It is worth remembering, however, that a key factor in David Cameron's successful leadership bid was his speech at the conference of 2005.

6.3 Leadership selection

Selection of the Conservative Party leader

Until 1965 the Conservative method of leadership selection involved discreet consultation among senior members of the party, with the monarch sometimes taking a view as well. It is known that the queen was influential in choosing, for example, Sir Alec Douglas-Home in 1963. The fact that many Conservatives saw him as a particularly incompetent leader led to demands to change a method that many considered inappropriate for a party in a twentieth-century democracy.

This system of leadership selection changed in 1965 to the one that chose William Hague in 1997. Selection was made only by Conservative MPs. No party members or parliamentary candidates were involved, but MPs were expected to consult and listen to local party members. If 10% of Conservative MPs wanted a leadership election, they could have one. There was then a series of ballots until one candidate achieved an overall majority of the votes of all Conservative MPs.

William Hague was elected by Conservative MPs in 1997, but he introduced changes that now permit party members to be involved in the final selection,

> Look at the major issues which occurred during the autumn conferences of the three major parties.

Get accurate details of how David Cameron was elected.

with all members having one vote. Iain Duncan Smith, Michael Howard and David Cameron were chosen by this method.

Selection of the Labour Party leader

Before 1983 the Labour Party leader was elected by a ballot process open only to Labour MPs. As part of a series of reforms intended to make the party more democratic after the election defeat of 1979, a system known as an electoral college was introduced.

In this electoral college system, one-third of the total vote in the college is given to MPs and MEPs, one-third to members of trade unions that are affiliated to the Labour Party, and one-third to ordinary party members. In both the unions and the constituency parties there is OMOV (one member, one vote). In the past, trade unions could vote on behalf of their members (known as the block vote), and this gave union leaders huge influence over who was elected Labour leader. One trade union leader might be able to cast several hundred thousand votes — but now each member of a union has to be balloted separately. This was the system used to elect Tony Blair.

Make sure you know all the details of how Gordon Brown's successor was elected.

Selection of the Liberal Democratic Party leader

The leader has to be an MP, and each member of the party is allowed one vote.

6.4 Selection of parliamentary candidates

Selection of Conservative Party candidates

Potential candidates, who are expected to be party members, usually apply to Conservative Central Office and go through a vetting process operated by the candidate selection officer, who is appointed by the party leader. This gives the party leader a lot of influence. Once checked by the party, applicants must pass a Parliamentary Assessment Board. If approved by the board, a possible candidate is then put on the 'approved list' of candidates. The approved candidate may apply for any advertised vacancy in a parliamentary constituency. Once on the list, applicants can apply to go on the 'Priority List' (50% of which have to be women candidates), and they will be encouraged to go for the more winnable seats.

The local constituency then shortlists the applicants (there can be a large number in a safe Conservative seat) and makes the final choice. There is limited scope for the ordinary party member to be involved in the process, as much of it is conducted by the executive council of the local Conservative Association. However, it is normal for members of the local association to select the candidate from the shortlisted group after the applicants have spoken to them and answered their questions.

How much should the choice of candidate be left to the local party?

Traditionally, Central Office has exercised only limited control over local associations and has intervened only selectively in local matters. But under David Cameron's leadership, he and the party have increasingly intervened as much as possible to ensure that more women and members of ethnic minorities are selected for winnable seats, in order to broaden the appeal of the party. This 'parachuting' can raise issues about party democracy and cause a lot of friction between local parties and the party's head office. As the 2010 election showed, such attempts to 'parachute' favoured candidates into winnable seats do not always work.

Selection of Labour Party candidates

A would-be Labour candidate must first join the party. Although the party's head office has an approved list of parliamentary candidates, local parties do not have to choose a candidate from it. Other local groups, such as trade unions, may also put forward candidates. The party's NEC imposes specific rules about who may be shortlisted: for example, there has to be at least one woman on a shortlist. Then all local members and members of affiliated unions are allowed one vote each.

However, there is now much less union influence over candidate selection and much more NEC and leadership control than before. Since 1995 the NEC has refused to accept some candidates chosen locally, and has even imposed its own candidates on some constituencies. This is a major change for the Labour Party, which had always allowed much greater local control than the Conservative Party did.

Increasing the ability of the leader and the NEC to decide on suitable candidates has been a major part of the Labour Party's 'modernisation' programme. Neil Kinnock and Tony Blair wanted to stop local constituencies choosing candidates from the radical or 'left' wing of the party and thereby alienating the middle-ground voter felt to be vital for Labour success in general elections. One of the best examples of this came in 2003, when the Labour Party expelled George Galloway, a Labour MP, for his support for Saddam Hussein and opposition to Tony Blair's Iraq policy, so he could not stand as a Labour candidate in 2005.

How democratic is the candidate selection process?

Democracy

One of the most difficult tasks facing the leadership of a political party — which is, of course, a vital part of the democratic process — is how democratic that party can be itself. Consider what is the most appropriate action for a democratically elected party leader to take when a tiny minority of party members choose parliamentary candidates who the leader believes will lead to the party losing seats or even the general election. Again there are concerns about 'parachuting' and imposing 'all-women' shortlists.

6.5 Funding of parties

The way in which political parties obtain the money needed to function has become a major issue in recent years. In the past, business largely funded the Conservative Party and the trade unions largely funded the Labour Party. Neither party got enough to survive solely from donations from members. Both parties were regularly criticised for being too dependent on a single source for their funding, and therefore likely to be too influenced when in government by the source of their funds. Labour governments were accused of favouring the 'working class', as the bulk of their funds came from the large public sector trade unions, such as the Post Office workers. The Conservative Party was criticised for being too 'boss' orientated, as it gained the bulk of its funding from major companies, such as the Commercial Union insurance company. Usually only a very small percentage of party income came from the membership, and in both major parties membership has been falling rapidly in recent decades. The Liberal Democrats rely largely on donations from individuals.

There is a growing expectation from the public of better performance by political parties, but parties face a decline in their income. As both unions and business are unhappy about the 'return' they have been getting on their investment, they are giving less money to the parties.

	Labour Party	Conservative Party	Liberal Democratic Party
1997	£26m	£28m	£2m
2001	£11m	£13m	£1m
2005	£14.9m	£14.2m	£5.3m

Table 4.1 Party election spending

	Labour Party	Conservative Party	Liberal Democratic Party
Total income in 2009	£16.2m	£32.5m	£6.2m
Income from public funds 2009	£1.07m	£5.4m	£2.3m
Donations in the first 3 months of 2010	£4.1m	£12.36m	£1.9m

Table 4.2 Party income

The above leads inevitably to the accusation that money can 'buy' elections. It was also felt to be very unfair on the Liberal Democrats that they could not compete with the two major parties, as they were unable to raise their profile without greater funding. They argued strongly that lack of funding deprived the electorate of a real 'choice'.

6.6 Reform of the funding of political parties

Several funding scandals that affected both parties ('Cash for Questions' and the Ecclestone affair) led to Tony Blair's government asking the Neill Committee on Standards in Public Life (initially set up by John Major) to look at the whole issue of the funding of political parties. The Neill Report recommended:

- no foreign donations — both major parties had been criticised for taking money from people abroad
- public knowledge of all large donations, so that at least the public would know who was funding parties
- a £20 million cap on spending by a party at general elections — this would ease the money-raising problems of the two major parties, but give little comfort to the Liberal Democrats and other small parties
- an increase in state funding, particularly for opposition parties
- that shareholders should approve company donations to a political party, in the same way that union members have to approve union donations to a political party
- fair funding for both 'sides' in referendums — it was felt that the government of the day was able to influence referendum results too easily

Although the report led to clear limits on election spending for the Scottish Parliament and Welsh Assembly elections in 1998, nothing has happened to implement these recommendations in other respects, and they did not apply to the election of 2001.

Note the impact of the 'cap' now imposed. The amount that can be spent in individual constituencies is also very tightly regulated. The Labour Party did not find it easy to raise this money, as trade unions such as the GMB have reduced their support in protest at some 'New' Labour policies. In addition, membership was down from over 400,000 in 1997 to about 180,000 in summer 2007, which reduced income severely.

The Labour Party is now increasingly dependent on donations from rich businessmen such as Lord Sainsbury (£8.5 million between 1999 and 2003) and Lord Paul, and is suffering from the sorts of criticism that Labour itself directed at the Conservatives in previous years. In addition to the funds that the two major parties spend on a general election centrally — on party political broadcasts, national advertising and leaders touring the country — parties are allowed to spend locally. For the 2001 election, every party was allowed to spend £5,483 and 6.2p per elector in a rural constituency, and slightly less in an urban one. The issue continues — as the Ashcroft and Paul and Unite affairs demonstrated in 2010.

Be prepared to argue the case for and against state funding of parties.

6.7 State funding of parties

The following arguments are made in favour of state funding of parties:
- It would remove the large sums that the two parties get from private donors, who might have sinister and selfish objectives in giving a party money.
- It would help the minority parties and eliminate the criticism that elections can be 'bought'.
- Parties perform such a vital role in a democracy that they really ought to be fairly and ethically funded.
- Many feel that the opposition is unable to do its work properly as it lacks the funding to research policy and provide an effective alternative to the government of the day.
- The leader of the opposition is paid, as is the opposition chief whip, and there is a small contribution towards running the leader of the opposition's office. However, the opposition shadow cabinet gets no assistance from the state.

There are, however, a number of arguments against the idea of state funding:
- How much a party should get would be difficult to work out.
- Many people might dislike the idea of their hard-earned tax money going to radical or extremist parties.
- The UK is a free society, and individuals who wish to give a large (or small) sum of money to a party should be free to do so.

6.8 The role of the party member

All parties are desperate for members, partly to get money from them and partly to have activists who will help get the vote out at election times. However the 'nationalisation' of politics and the tendency of parties to raise money from

'big' donors have lessened the importance of the party member. Also, active party members tend to come from the more radical wings of a party, such as the left in Labour or the right in the Conservatives, and tend to advocate the sort of policies — such as nationalisation (Labour) or hanging (the Conservatives) — which the leadership feels might be election losers. The ways in which party members can participate are:

- choosing the party leader
- choosing party candidates
- easy access to MP or councillor
- conference attendance
- influencing party policy
- canvassing and leafleting at election time

> Why are so few people joining political parties now?

6.9 Party systems

You need to be aware of the various types of party system and the differences between them. There are four main types:

The one-party system

Only one party is allowed: others are banned. Membership of that party is critical for promotion. This system is often a vehicle for one-person rule, as in Germany under the Nazi party.

The two-party system

Only two parties stand any chance of success. This could have applied to the UK from 1945 onwards (until 2010) and applies to the USA at present. The two parties regularly alternate in power, with the 'out' party forming the official opposition.

The dominant party system

Only one party stands a chance of winning, but others are permitted. With no challenge, the party tends to split into factions, such as the 'wets' and 'drys' of the Conservatives, and 'New' and 'Old' Labour. This term could be applied to the Conservatives between 1979 and 1997, or Labour from 1997 to 2010.

Multi-party systems

More than two parties stand a chance of winning or forming part of a coalition government (as in Scotland, for example). Coalitions are the rule and not the exception. The rise of the Liberal Democrats in 2010 changed the scene in the UK. Proportional representation tends to lead to this system, while first past the post tends to lead to two-party systems.

Pressure groups are a compulsory topic for all boards. For OCR, where you have to do a question on pressure groups, make sure you have a really good knowledge of them.

To do well on this topic you need to:
- make sure you can define the different types of pressure groups and explain the part they play in UK politics
- make sure you have a good range of recent examples of pressure groups of different types and examples of them in action. Take care to research your own examples (most pressure groups have good websites, so it is easy). This is vital. So many answers in examinations simply list broad points and don't give examples to back them up. It is often the right example that makes it clear that you know what you are talking about
- make sure you can develop clear arguments each way on the merits and demerits of pressure groups and cope with all the discursive questions set out below

Get your own recent examples of pressure groups at work.

Short questions

1 Describe the differences between a pressure group and a political party.
2 What are the functions of a pressure group?
3 Explain, with examples, what are (a) sectional, (b) promotional, (c) insider, (d) outsider pressure groups.
4 What factors affect pressure group influence?

Essay questions

5 Do pressure groups have too much influence?
6 Are pressure groups a threat to democracy?
7 Analyse the factors which influence pressure group success.
8 To what extent do pressure groups promote political participation and responsive government?

1 What is a pressure group?

1.1 Definition

A pressure group is an organised group of people who get together to achieve an objective. This might be trying to stop a new runway being built at Heathrow (NoTRAG) or preventing cruelty to children (the NSPCC). They usually do not stand for election to Parliament or a local council, but just hope to **influence** the government or other decision makers.

Influence: the ability to affect decisions through persuasion. It is what pressure groups do, or try to do.

Pressure: the application by groups or individuals of organised persuasion with the intention of affecting decision making.

1.2 Pressure groups and political parties

It is important to understand the differences between a political party and a pressure group. A political party actively seeks to become the government, not just to influence it. **Pressure** groups just want to influence government or change attitudes. Sometimes a pressure group will put up candidates for election in order to gain publicity and make a point — a good example of this is the 'Save Kidderminster Hospital' pressure group, which put up Dr Richard Taylor as a candidate for Kidderminster in 2001: he won the seat in the House of Commons. The Green movement won its first seat in the Commons in 2010.

2 *Types of pressure group*

Political scientists tend to use different words to classify the various types of pressure group. Some will call them 'interest' groups instead. There are different names, such as:

- promotional groups
- peak associations
- episodic groups
- 'fire brigade' groups
- single-cause/multi-cause groups
- protective groups

Be able to define, and give examples of, the different types of pressure group.

The best advice is to learn the four main groups described below, as these are universally accepted (particularly by examiners).

2.1 Insider groups

These are pressure groups which the government sees as respectable, responsible and well informed, and with which it likes to be associated. Insider groups are usually given direct and frequent access to ministers and their departments. If a new law or major new policy is being considered by a government, the insider group would expect to be consulted by government and have its views taken very seriously. They usually give specialist advice to government, have the confidence of the public and government, and are reluctant to go against the main policies and strategies of government. They are more likely to compromise with government in order to retain their insider status.

Examples of insider pressure groups are the British Medical Association, the Police Federation, and the National Farmers' Union.

There can be risks to the public/democratic process if a government allows too much insider status to a pressure group. Some people argue that the interests of patients and taxpayers might be neglected if, for example, the British Medical Association gets too close to the government, or the interests of consumers and taxpayers could be downplayed if the National Farmers' Union has too much influence.

2.2 Outsider groups

These are groups that do not wish to be too closely associated with government, are unable to gain any formal recognition from government, or are advocating a policy which strongly conflicts with government policy.

Examples of outsider pressure groups are the Campaign for Nuclear Disarmament, the Prison Reform Trust and Liberty.

Some outsider groups would like to become insider groups in order to have more influence, such as the Terence Higgins Trust, which helps those with AIDS. Other outsider groups, such as the Prison Reform Trust, might like to have more influence, but as they represent a group (current and former prisoners) with which the public and government do not have much sympathy, they are likely to be kept as outsiders.

> Get examples of pressure groups influencing thinking rather than actually making something happen.

2.3 Sectional groups

These represent a particular section of society, such as motor manufacturers, teachers, lawyers or patients. They aim to look after the interests of that particular group and perhaps stop things happening to that particular group which might harm their interests. For example, the Patients' Association objected to the removal of a patient's right to see their medical records or the discontinuation of the requirement for GPs to provide an out-of-hours service. Sectional groups will also try to make things happen which will benefit their group, such as maintaining a good pension scheme for postal workers (Communication Workers Union). Examples of sectional groups are:

- the Law Society/the Bar Council (lawyers)
- the British Medical Association (doctors)
- the National Union of Students

Some people express concern that if such groups gain too much influence, the interests that they represent could harm the interests of the wider public.

2.4 Cause or promotional groups

There are two main types of cause or promotional group. One is a group set up to achieve a single limited objective, such as to stop a third runway being built at Heathrow. The other has a broader and more long-term objective, such as the Child Poverty Action Group, which campaigns to end child poverty. Examples of such groups are:

- the Campaign for Nuclear Disarmament
- Greenpeace
- Fathers4Justice
- abortion rights/the 20 weeks campaign

While some of these groups can bring wide-ranging benefits, such as the NSPCC, some would argue that others can be selfish and unaware of wider issues. Those who want another runway at Heathrow, for example, argue that it would help employment, business and tourism.

3 *The role and functions of pressure groups*

Pressure groups perform a vital role in our democratic process. If we did not tolerate and encourage pressure groups, we could not call ourselves a democracy.

3.1 Positive functions

Try to envisage politics without pressure groups.

- They enable individuals to participate in the national political process between elections. For example, you can join a group to ban foxhunting even though you might have voted for an MP or party that favours it. Pressure groups give citizens another voice in the decision-making process.
- They are a useful way for individuals to participate in local and national politics, besides voting. Pressure groups are formed to try to persuade a council to keep open a village school, for example, or to persuade the local planning committee to refuse permission for a branch of McDonald's or Tesco to open in an area.
- They ensure that minorities, such as homosexuals, people with AIDS or those who wish to close all shops on Sundays, can make their voice heard. They help to prevent a 'tyranny of the majority', where the majority impose possibly intolerant policies on a minority group in the community.
- They make the government aware of views other than those coming through the political parties or the civil service. For example, the 'official' view is that genetically modified crops, widely grown in the USA, are perfectly safe. However, certain pressure groups in the UK have hindered their development (sometimes using illegal methods) and insisted that there should be further debate on the issue. Whether it is 'democratic' for such a minority to hold back what other people might see as real progress is an important question to debate.
- They can bring expert knowledge to the government's attention on an important issue. For example, the Royal Society for the Prevention of Accidents (RoSPA), whose membership includes many very experienced casualty doctors and health and safety experts, has played a major role in making cars and our roads safer by providing government with expert advice.
- They can generate new ideas that practising politicians often do not have time to consider. This type of pressure group is sometimes known as a 'think-tank'. Good examples of these are the Institute for Public Policy Research, Demos and Compass, which had a lot of influence on New Labour thinking, and the Policy Exchange, Reform and the Centre For Policy Studies, which have a lot of influence on Conservative ideas.
- They enable groups that are not seen as electorally important, such as students, to make their views known.
- They perform a useful scrutiny function. It does no harm for decision takers at all levels to know there could be a well-organised and informed group monitoring their actions.
- They have a good safety-valve function — they provide an outlet between elections for the public to make their views known.
- They provide a good means of participation in politics as well as a way of encouraging the dispersal of power away from the centre.

- They encourage informed debate on issues. While NoTRAG argues the case against a third runway at Heathrow, pressure groups representing the airlines, passengers, local industries and tourism argue the case for. Pressure groups can balance each other out.

3.2 Functions which can be seen as harmful

How strong is the case for regulating pressure groups?

Pressure groups can harm the democratic process in several ways:

- They can be sectional and selfish. One powerful group can dominate an issue, such as healthcare. The GPs and consultants are very powerfully organised, and nurses and patients may lose out as a result.
- They can be so skilled at putting pressure on ministers and Parliament that the latter forget the interests of the general public. For example, in the cases of salmonella in eggs and BSE in cows, it is argued that the health interests of the general public were not the primary concern of ministers and civil servants. The interests of farmers and the NFU were seen as more important.
- A few elite groups dominate society — as one writer put it, 'in pluralist heaven the heavenly choir sings with a strong upper-class accent'. The Bar Council, which looks after the interests of barristers, is a good example here. Many critics of the legal system, with its high costs and slowness, and the need to employ both a solicitor and a barrister in major cases, feel that the Bar Council's dominant position is a barrier to reform. The large number of lawyers in politics is sometimes felt to prevent law reforms that would be in the public interest.
- Pressure groups are very good at stopping activities which other people may feel are needed. When the building of the M42 was held up by pressure groups for 14 years, Midlands industry and employment were estimated to have suffered considerably as a result. Animal rights groups came close to shutting down the Huntingdon Life Sciences firm, which tested drugs on animals prior to their use on humans. Drugs firms (through their own pressure groups) argued that major health benefits to humans would be blocked if their products were not tested on animals, and that jobs and wealth would be lost in the UK if the firm closed and the work were carried out abroad.
- They can cause social disharmony, as those groups that are not well organised lose out to those that are. Consider the conflict between the Lord's Day Observance Society and the supermarkets over Sunday trading. Shops that wished to open on Sunday organised themselves into a very powerful pressure group and raised a lot of money to pressurise Parliament to change the law. The Lord's Day Observance Society simply could not match their resources, although polls at the time indicated a fair amount of popular support for their cause. The retail trade unions, who opposed Sunday opening on behalf of their members, also could not match the resources of the supermarkets. The majority of those union members opposed the change. Supermarkets, needless to say, are open on Sundays.

How easy would it be to regulate pressure groups in a democracy?

- Small numbers of people who are not elected or really representative of the membership dominate some groups. The non-elected leadership of one of the motoring organisations, for example, opposed the compulsory wearing of seat belts, but a newspaper poll of the organisation's members revealed overwhelming support for the measure.

- They can be very undemocratic in structure. Not all have elections for senior positions, and a single powerful individual can dominate with their own particular agenda and methodology.
- They are not regulated in any way.
- Rich pressure groups can afford to hire the best PR companies, lawyers and professional lobby organisations which employ ex-ministers, civil servants and generals — and win.

Make sure you can argue a case each way on whether pressure groups are, or are not, a threat to the democratic process. Be prepared to get off the fence and give your reasons for arguing for one side in particular.

4 *Pressure group methods*

Pressure groups tend to use different methods at different times to achieve their objectives. Look at the methods outlined below for an essay such as 'Discuss the methods which are most likely to lead to pressure groups' success'.

Seeking to influence the government directly
Pressure groups may try to get access to the key decision makers — the prime minister, cabinet ministers and civil servants — and argue their case directly.

Seeking to influence MPs
They may try to influence MPs either individually or collectively, or target members of specific standing or select committees or parties. A good example is when Charter 88, a pressure group wanting major constitutional reform, targeted Labour MPs, candidates and party members in 1996–97 to get constitutional reform into the 1997 Labour manifesto. Another is when David Steel's Abortion Bill, legalising abortion, went through the committee stage in the House of Commons. Pressure groups ensured it was amended so that Roman Catholic nurses and doctors were not compelled to undertake tasks they found morally repugnant. It was also a pressure group which persuaded David Steel to put forward the Bill in the first place..

Seeking to influence members of the House of Lords
This is particularly likely when the Lords are debating or revising bills that have come up from the Commons. The many financial benefits that organisations dealing with the housing of the elderly get are mainly due to an alliance of pressure groups (e.g. Help the Aged) persuading members of the House of Lords to make certain amendments to the Housing Finance Act, and then persuading the House of Commons to accept those amendments.

Targeting political parties
Look at the number of pressure groups present at all major party conferences. Getting an issue onto a conference agenda, and possibly into a party's manifesto, can be vital.

Targeting MEPs and using the machinery of the EU
In many areas, such as agriculture and trade, where decisions are made in Brussels, direct contact with the relevant Commission and MEPs can be very important. The decision-making process in the EU is designed to be responsive

Evaluate the effectiveness of different pressure group methods

to pressure groups. Many major pressure groups, such as the National Farmers' Union, have offices in Brussels.

Seeking to influence key local officials

These include planning officers and local councillors. With the low turnout in local elections, local councillors tend to be very responsive to pressure groups which represent even a modest number of potential electors.

Launching a major media campaign

One example is the Snowdrop Campaign over the Dunblane massacre and gun control. Look also at the effect of the mass media on the fuel price protest in autumn 2000. Newspapers spend little on their own reporters and research and are often willing to have stories written for them by pressure groups.

Advertising

There is considerable disagreement about how effective advertising might be, but major groups such as Greenpeace and animal rights groups use it extensively at times. ASH, the anti-smoking pressure group, is another group that uses advertising extensively. An interesting exercise is to consider why ASH could be seen as an unsuccessful pressure group.

Hiring professional lobbyists

These **lobbyists** specialise in influencing government. It is accepted that one of the reasons why the £5 billion contract to maintain the UK's nuclear submarines went to Devonport and not Rosyth in Scotland was the millions that Devonport spent in hiring a company specialising in pressurising government (and with quite a lot of MPs on its payroll as 'consultants'). There is often a concern because some of these organisations hire ex-ministers and former high-ranking military officers or civil servants, as they have the 'right' contacts.

Phone-ins and online petitions

Making effective use of modern technology is proving increasingly effective.

Legal methods of protest

These methods include marches and demonstrations, such as the Countryside Alliance demonstration in London, and more forceful tactics, such as strikes and boycotts. There have been far fewer of the latter in recent years.

Illegal activities

Some pressure groups, such as several of the animal rights groups, use violence, civil disobedience and other illegal activities to further their cause. Try buying a genuine animal fur coat to see how effective illegality can be.

Be prepared to evaluate pressure group methods. Which method is most likely to lead to success for a particular type of group or cause?

5 *Factors which can lead to pressure group success*

This is one of the most difficult questions to answer. The Snowdrop Campaign to ban handguns in the UK probably succeeded simply because so many children were killed. There was such a feeling of revulsion nationally that no politician dared stand in the way of the ban on handguns, or listen to the views of the pro-gun pressure group that wanted to keep handguns for clubs.

Lobbying: to lobby is to make direct contact with a policy maker in order to try to influence them. A lobbyist is the person making the contact.

Analyse how important money is to pressure group effectiveness.

Reasons to consider are as follows:

- The support of the media, particularly if it is sustained over a period of time. Also the way in which a pressure group uses the media can be critical.
- The sympathy the government feels for the issue and how many votes it feels it might win or lose. The nearness of an election may well be a factor here.
- The question of whether decision makers are in broad agreement with the pressure group.
- The size and possible electoral impact of the group's membership.
- How united the pressure group is (e.g. teachers have at least six different unions that frequently disagree, whereas GPs have one, the BMA, and so the latter is much more likely to be listened to).
- Whether the pressure group has the resources to employ able managers, to advertise etc. Money can be vital.
- The quality of the group's organisation and leadership, and whether the pressure group chooses the right methods and targets the right people.
- The attitude of the public towards the issue (e.g. an environmental disaster will help environmental groups).
- The pressure group's ability to make alliances with other groups over an issue. Coalitions of groups can often be successful.
- The number of members the group has, and the type of membership. A mass group such as the RSPB will carry a lot of weight. Having the 'right' sort of membership helps as well. Hospital consultants are much more likely to be listened to than hospital porters.
- The ability to cause trouble. Fuel tanker drivers and firefighters are much more likely to be listened to than florists.

Be prepared for a question such as, 'Why are some pressure groups more successful than others?'.

6 The reasons for pressure group growth

Be prepared to explain why pressure groups are growing in both number and influence (and are forming a bigger part of Government and Politics courses!).

- There is more government, covering more areas affecting individuals, such as child support and child protection, so those individuals affected will want to organise to influence relevant decision taking.
- With much greater centralisation of power in London in areas such as education, there are no longer local decision takers who can easily be contacted or influenced. So there have to be nationally organised campaigns to influence central government.
- Communication has become increasingly easier and cheaper. Look at the impact of e-mail and blogs on pressure group success.
- The decline of parties and party membership. Pressure groups are the way in which individuals can influence the policy makers.
- There is now a multicultural and multiethnic society, and its varied citizenship is looking for representation of a type that the mass political parties can no longer give.
- The evidence of success of pressure groups, from the anti-slavery movement and the suffragettes to the NFU (farmers still don't pay council tax) and the Bar Council, encourages people to join.

Analyse how important insider status is to pressure group effectiveness.

How important has modern technology been to pressure group growth?

7 ## The impact of UK membership of the EU on pressure groups

There is an increasing number of areas, ranging from working conditions to farmers' milk quotas, where the EU makes the rules for us all. Pressure groups quickly realised that effective organisation in, and focus on, the EU decision-making process could lead to success for their cause.

The reasons why membership of the EU has had an impact on pressure group success are as follows:
- The key policy makers, the Commission, are small in number, easily targeted and accessible.
- The relevant UK representatives, such as those on the Council of Ministers (the decision takers) are also few in numbers, known to all, and accessible.
- MEPs and the European Parliament (who have a growing influence on EU legislation and its implementation) are accessible and expect to utilise pressure groups.
- The whole policy and decision-making process within the EU is accessible to pressure groups, and pressure groups are expected to participate in the policy-making process.

> Note how membership of the EU has impacted on UK pressure groups

This is why many pressure groups have utilised the EU successfully and have offices in Brussels.

Pressure groups have also used the European Court of Human Rights and the European Court of Justice (do not confuse the two) to attain their objectives.

Good examples of effective use of the EU structure to gain objectives are:
- animal welfare, particularly in areas such as the slaughtering and transport of animals
- equal pay and conditions for women

8 ## Pressure group theory

> Pluralism: literally, holding more than one idea or doing more than one thing. Pressure groups encourage pluralism, diversity and representation in a democratic society, as a citizen can vote Labour, for instance, but also join a pressure group that campaigns to keep foxhunting.

An outline grasp of pressure group theory can very useful for high AO2 marks. The theory will be very important for A2 work. There are four main 'theories'.

8.1 The Pluralist theory

This is the prevailing theory. It argues that pressure groups:
- are beneficial
- involve ordinary citizens, so are democratic
- bring skills and expertise to bear on an issue
- represent minorities
- prevent one group from dominating a debate
- bring diverse influences into decision making
- disperse power away from centres

(Get your own examples to illustrate the points above.)

> Pluralist democracy: a democracy which recognises, accepts and acts inclusively towards all different types of organisations and interests.

Corporatism:
a system where
recognised interest
(pressure) groups such
as trade unions and
manufacturers work
with government to
make policy and help
implement that policy.

8.2 The Corporatist theory

Some argue that this 'theory' was actually put into practice in the UK from the 1950 to the 1970s. It sees pressure groups as largely beneficial organisations, since:

- government shares power with groups in return for those groups' support for government policy
- government, management and unions decide on economic and social policy
- management and unions (both pressure groups) play a role in implementing policy, such as controlling prices and wages

8.3 The New Right theory

This argues that:

- pressure groups bring few benefits and possibly do much harm
- pressure groups are essentially selfish and harm the national 'good'
- the current situation leads to the domination of producer interests, such as the supermarkets and the bankers
- the current situation is leading to the decline of the UK, as narrow and self-interested groups are dominating the decision-making process
- the 'closed-shop' policy of unions and the selfish interests of groups such as lawyers are not good for the country

If you are really aiming
for an A* grade, make
sure you grasp pressure
group 'theory'.

8.4 The Marxist theory

This theory:

- sees pressure groups as dangerous and undemocratic
- feels that pressure groups are dominated by producer groups and capitalists
- argues that too little power goes to the people

Note that the issue of pressure politics featured in the 2010 election campaign, as parties suggested a register for all pressure groups to bring more transparency into pressure politics. There had been a serious concern that too many former politicians, civil servants and military personnel were leaving their jobs and going to work for lobbying firms, making 'unfair' use of their former colleagues and contacts. A television programme caught several leading politicians offering their contacts and insider knowledge to a lobbying firm in return for cash in 2010.

This is a compulsory topic for both Edexcel and AQA. OCR has it as an optional topic, but some constitutional knowledge may well be needed for other topics. OCR's questions will only be essay ones, requiring both analysis and knowledge, while Edexcel's and AQA's questions could be either short or essay ones.

To do well in the examination you need to:

- make sure you are able to explain concepts and terms, such as 'federalism' or a 'rigid' constitution
- be fully up to date on recent constitutional changes and the current debate on the constitution — constitutional issues featured largely in the 2010 election campaign and the coalition government made major changes, such as introducing fixed-term parliaments

Staying up to date on the changes since 2010 is vital

Short questions

1 Explain what is meant by:
   - a rigid constitution
   - an uncodified constitution
   - a unitary constitution
2 Describe the principal sources of the UK constitution.
3 Explain what is meant by the separation of powers.
4 Explain what is meant by a constitutional convention.

Essay questions

5 Analyse to what extent the UK constitution influences and limits the powers of government.
6 Make out a case for and against a written constitution.
7 How strong is the case for further reform of the UK constitution?
8 To what extent did the Labour governments of 1997–2010 radically change the constitution?

1 Definition of a constitution

A constitution is primarily a set of rules specifying how a country should be governed. Constitutions such as those in France and the USA clearly lay down in writing the powers that the president has, how he or she can be removed, and the president's relationship with the legislative body (parliament) in that country. Matters such as those listed below are usually contained in a constitution:

- Elections — how they are conducted.
- The relationship between the executive, legislative and judicial parts of government. For example, it is usual to set out the exact powers of the prime minister/president, and how the incumbent can be checked or removed.
- Usually a statement as to where sovereignty (final power) lies. In the case of the USA, it lies with the people.

- Ways in which the constitution can be changed.
- A list of what rights citizens have. In the case of the USA, the first ten amendments (changes) to the constitution are known as the Bill of Rights, which guarantees freedoms such as the right to a proper trial.
- The overall type of government. The US Constitution specifies that it will be both a democratic and a federal system.

1.1 The role and function of a constitution

- To provide a clear set of rules for both government and citizen.
- To protect freedoms and to give limits to the power of government and police.
- To make clear the underlying principles of a state — for example, it is a republic, or democratic, or Catholic.
- To make it clear where power lies in a federal system — for example, where local government may have certain specific powers.
- To give legitimacy to the work of the state.

Do not confuse the sources with the underlying principles.

2 *The main sources of the UK constitution*

If the UK, unlike most other countries, does not have a written constitution, then certain questions arise:
- How do the country's citizens know what the rules are?
- Where have the rules that run the UK come from?
- Can these rules be changed?
- If so, how can they be changed?

It is not difficult to write down what the main rules are. For example, when a party wins a general election, the constitutional 'rule' is that the leader of that party is asked by the monarch to be the prime minister.

As it happens, there is no piece of paper giving the job specification of a prime minister (whose formal title is First Lord of the Treasury). Everyone accepts the constitutional 'rule' that it is now the prime minister's job to ask some senior colleagues of the same winning party (who must be members of Parliament — another unwritten rule) to join the cabinet.

Where does the prime minister get the authority to do all this?

The main sources, or origins, of our constitutional rules are:
- the traditional powers of Medieval monarchs, known as the royal prerogatives
- conventions
- common law
- statute law
- written works by well-known experts on the 'constitution'
- the rules of international organisations to which the UK now belongs, such as the EU

These are all explained in detail below.

2.1 Royal prerogatives

Note how many of the major powers of the prime minister have come from the royal prerogative.

These were the powers that Medieval monarchs had, before the days of Parliament. They included the powers:

- to declare war or make peace
- to command armies and appoint generals to fight for the monarch
- to appoint ministers
- to raise the money to pay for soldiers and ministers
- to appoint judges and maintain law and order

These were the powers that it was felt necessary for a monarch to have in order to defend his or her people and ensure their well-being. Over the centuries they have passed from monarch to prime minister, a situation perhaps best illustrated in 1936 when the prime minister, Stanley Baldwin, told the king, Edward VIII, that if he chose to marry the divorced Mrs Simpson he would have to abdicate. Tony Blair might have informed the queen that he was sending 'her' troops into Kosovo, but he certainly would not have consulted her.

Here are some further examples of the traditional royal prerogative being used by the prime minister:

- Tony Blair's decision to invade Iraq.
- John Major's negotiation of the Maastricht Treaty.
- Gordon Brown's decision to have a general election in 2010 and not in 2008.
- Brown's decision to reshuffle his cabinet after becoming prime minister.

2.2 Conventions

The best definition of a convention is that it is an unwritten rule or custom, which is known to all, accepted by all, and followed by all. 'Ministerial responsibility' is a good example of this. There is no law which lays down that a minister is responsible for everything his or her department does, but all ministers accept it. A further part of this convention is that if a minister makes a major error of judgement, he or she will resign. A good example of this is that when Peter Mandelson, secretary of state for trade and industry, was discovered to have 'forgotten' to declare the loan of a large sum of money from another minister to buy a house, he resigned.

Here are some other examples of important constitutional conventions:

- The whole cabinet takes collective responsibility for, and supports in public, a decision made by any member of the cabinet.
- The monarch accepts the advice of the prime minister.
- The monarch always signs bills that are agreed by both Houses of Parliament.
- Major changes to the constitution, such as **devolution**, will be put to a referendum before Parliament acts on them.

Devolution: the system whereby certain powers, e.g. control over education, are passed from the sovereign body, such as the UK Parliament, to another, such as the Scottish Parliament. They can, however, be taken back.

2.3 Common law

This is law based on the rulings made by judges in cases where there is no clear statute law (see below). For example, it was a judge who ruled that defendants had a right to silence in criminal cases. It was another judge who ruled in the 1770s that slavery could not exist in Britain.

Be able to explain
clearly the difference
between common
law and statute law.

Many of these rulings by judges gave UK citizens the rights that are normally laid down in written constitutions. Their decisions became part of the rules that affect the way in which the UK is governed.

2.4 Statute law

This is law passed by both Houses of Parliament and signed by the monarch. As early as 1500 everyone accepted that this was the supreme form of law and could overrule, for example, the wishes of the monarch or a custom that had been observed for centuries. The courts, the police and the government must enforce this type of law, which is known as an Act of Parliament when agreed by all three parts of Parliament: the Commons, the Lords and the monarch. A large number of Acts play a very important part in making up the constitution. Examples are:

- the Mutiny Act, which gives military officers the right to give orders to and discipline soldiers
- the Parliament Act, which rules that there has to be a general election at least every 5 years
- the Human Rights Act, which guarantees many basic freedoms

Everyone must obey all these Acts, many of which are normally written into the constitutions of other countries.

2.5 Written works by constitutional experts

These are books by accepted experts on the constitution, or parts of it. Very often they simply contain what everyone knows is supposed to happen, but they do it in a clear form so that newcomers to politics and government can actually read 'the constitution'.

- A good example of this is Bagehot's *The English Constitution*, written in the second half of the nineteenth century. He describes clearly what the role of the cabinet, Parliament and the monarch then was. What he did was put on paper what everyone knew was right in practice.
- Other important texts are Erskine May's *Parliamentary Practice*, which explains how Parliament works, and Dicey's *Introduction to the Study of the Law of the Constitution*, which analyses in depth such areas as the exact relationship between judges and the government.

2.6 Membership of international organisations such as the EU

Note the huge impact
that membership
of the EU has on
our constitution.

Membership of the EU has also altered the UK constitution. When we joined it, we accepted that some of the rules by which we are governed would now be made in Brussels. We agreed to give up our sovereignty in specified areas in order to gain the benefits of membership of this 'club'.

In the past, we accepted that the UK Parliament was sovereign in all matters. Then, by passing a statute law, Parliament changed the UK constitution to give the EU some powers to make rules that bind all UK citizens. The EU now decides the size of lorries allowed on our roads, for example. Other European countries, such as Ireland, can only change their constitution by a referendum in which all the people of that country are consulted, while in the UK the constitution can be changed just by passing an Act of Parliament.

3 *Principles of the UK constitution*

In the USA, the constitution states that the reason for the constitution's existence is to enable the American people to have 'life, liberty and the pursuit of happiness'. With no written constitution in the UK, there is a debate about what the underlying principles and purpose of the unwritten UK constitution are. In theory, however, they are supposed to be:

- the sovereignty of Parliament
- the **rule of law**
- the unitary state
- the separation of powers
- responsible government

Rule of law: simply, 'the law rules'. Everyone is under the law and must obey it regardless of their status. Laws must be interpreted and applied by an independent and impartial judiciary.

3.1 The sovereignty of Parliament

Quite simply this means that the UK Parliament is the UK's sovereign body. This means that it has absolute power over everyone in the country. It can pass a law enabling the UK to join the EU, but it can pass a law that takes it out again. It can bring back capital punishment and allow the state to execute citizens, or it can take away the right of a woman to have an abortion. Now that specific powers have been given to the Scottish Parliament and to the European Commission, Parliament has reduced its sovereignty, but can regain it fully if it wishes.

The use of referendums to consult people, instead of Parliament just taking the decisions, may also have reduced Parliament's sovereignty. However, there is nothing in the UK constitution to make Parliament call more referendums.

Be able to explain clearly when constitutional theory differs from what is actually happening.

3.2 The rule of law

Quite simply this means that 'law rules'. It also means that in the UK all citizens are under the law, and that includes the monarch and members of the government. All must obey the law and all should be equal before it. Government, the police and everyone acting in an official capacity must obey the law and recognise the legal rights of the people they are supposed to be serving. This means that all accused citizens are entitled to their day in court, and to have a fair trial. It also means that a citizen can take members of the government to court if they believe they have acted against the law or exceeded the powers that Parliament gave them. It also states that judges ought to be independent from political control, and should obey the law and not the government.

3.3 The unitary state

A unitary state is a state where one body holds all the important powers. In the case of the UK, this is Parliament and the government in London. Whatever powers might be given to other bodies, say to the mayor of London or the Scottish Parliament, are given by Parliament and can be taken away again. However, note the changes resulting from the devolution of powers to the Scottish Parliament and to the EU. The principle of the unitary state is evidently decreasing in importance.

3.4 The separation of powers

This is an old idea that is fine in theory but which never seems to have actually worked in practice in the UK. The idea was originally that the three 'powers' — the executive, the legislature and the judiciary — should always be quite separate. No one person should be a member of more than one of these parts of government. The idea was that for citizens to have freedom and protection from a bad government, an incompetent Parliament or a biased judge, each of the three parts should have a checking role on the others. Parliament, for example, could get rid of a bad judge or an incompetent minister; a judge could imprison a corrupt minister.

However, practice is now divorced from theory in that, by convention, government ministers all sit in Parliament and the Lord Chancellor/secretary of state for justice has responsibility for the management of the court system.

Note the impact of the Constitutional Reform Act on the separation of powers in the UK.

3.5 Responsible government

This principle is derived from two conventions mentioned earlier: ministerial responsibility and collective cabinet responsibility. It means that the government must take responsibility for its actions. The right of citizens to call a minister to account for his or her actions is a vital part of democracy in the UK. This is also known as the principle of accountability.

4 The constitution as an issue

The constitution has become an important issue in recent years. Since about 1970 many different groups have suggested that the constitution should be both changed and written down clearly. There are many reasons for this. The main ones are:

- a growing dislike of UK methods of election, which many saw as 'unfair'
- the fact that no party since the Second World War has had a majority of the electorate vote for it
- growing demands by people in Scotland, Wales and Northern Ireland for less control from London
- a growing dislike of the role and influence of the unelected monarchy and the unelected House of Lords
- the changes membership of the EU brought by to the UK system of government
- a growing concern that individual liberty was being reduced and that the government was growing too powerful
- a genuine wish to have a clear, simple and written constitution that everyone knew and understood

4.1 Recent constitutional changes

The Labour government first elected in 1997 had promised in its manifesto to make constitutional changes. It delivered on some of its promises, but its

critics argued that it did not go as far as it should have. The changes it made (by statute) are as follows:

- It reformed the House of Lords. The right of the hereditary peers to sit and vote in the House of Lords was abolished.
- It devolved power to Scotland, Wales and Northern Ireland. Scotland has its own Parliament, and Wales and Northern Ireland their own assemblies.
- It altered the electoral system in Scotland, Wales and Northern Ireland. Proportional representation was introduced.
- It held binding referendums in Scotland, Wales and Northern Ireland.
- It brought in the Human Rights Act, which guarantees liberties to citizens.
- It set up the new post of mayor of London, with devolved powers.
- It changed the relationship between the executive and the judiciary in the Constitutional Reform Act of 2005.
- It passed the Freedom of Information Act.
- It passed the Political Parties, Elections and Referendums Act, which reformed all three areas.
- It ratified the Amsterdam, Nice and Lisbon Treaties, which further affected the UK's relationship with the EU.

The general election of 2010 and the coalition government which resulted from it have also led to major changes affecting the constitution, such as a move to fixed-term elections.

4.2 Criticisms of the Labour government's constitutional changes

- The Labour government did not reform the House of Commons in a meaningful way. It had been suggested that the government would give select committees much more power to scrutinise the executive and also make Parliament work more sensible hours and not late at night. These changes did not happen. In fact, the government increased its hold and influence over Parliament, and it has been argued that it largely ignored Parliament because it had such a large majority in the Commons.
- It did not change the voting system for general elections in the UK. Tony Blair failed to get a majority of the electorate to vote for him in 2001, yet he still had a huge majority in the Commons.
- It did not fully tackle the problem of the House of Lords. It did not reform the role of the Lords. Peers remained unelected, and many of those appointed seemed to be strong supporters of the Labour government.
- It did not really sort out the relationship between the government in London and those in Edinburgh, Cardiff and Belfast.
- There is still no written constitution in the UK.

5 # The debate on the constitution — the party manifestos in 2005

The constitution remained a feature in all manifestos in the 2005 general election, but not to the extent it had been in 1997.

The Labour Party said it would:
- complete the reform of the House of Lords
- embed and extend devolution
- promote more self-government in local communities
- encourage more directly elected mayors

The Conservative Party said it would:
- ensure that English laws would be decided by English voters
- have no regional assemblies
- have a stronger Parliament
- liberate local government
- oppose any EU constitution and work towards the EU becoming more 'decentralised'

The Liberal Democratic Party would:
- bring in electoral reform
- reform the House of Lords totally
- cut government departments
- extend devolution substantially
- increase parliamentary oversight of the executive
- move towards a **federal** Europe

When Gordon Brown succeeded Tony Blair as prime minister, those who wished for further constitutional changes hoped for action, since he had made major speeches on the need for reform in 1992 and 1997, and in his party leadership campaign he said he wanted to 'build a shared national consensus for a programme of constitutional reform'. The main reforms he indicated he wished to make were:
- protection for the individual against the state
- increased accountability for public officials
- reduction of the prime minister's powers of patronage
- reduction of the royal prerogative in areas such as the declaration of war
- introduction of a Bill of Rights
- further reform of the Lords
- changes to the funding of political parties
- devolution
- granting of greater scrutiny powers to Parliament
- possible electoral reform
- extending the scope of the Freedom of Information Act

However, with the onset of the economic crisis in 2008 no major advance had been made by the dissolution of Parliament in 2010.

5.1 Should the UK have a written constitution?

This debate has been going on for decades, and is also a likely question.

The main arguments for:
- Everyone would know exactly what a government can and cannot do.
- It would prevent government from becoming too powerful.
- It would give the UK the opportunity to get rid of out-of-date parts of its constitution, such as a hereditary monarchy.

Federal state: a state in which power is divided between national and local governments, each having authority over specific areas, such as foreign policy or education.

- Everyone would know their rights.
- It would end the odd system where the underlying theories, such as the separation of powers, do not match up with current practice.

Arguments against:
- The present system actually works well — it is flexible and people like it.
- There is no demand for much change.
- There would be no real agreement on what should replace the existing system.
- We would lose the great flexibility we have: we can change the rules quickly if we want to.
- Other countries with **rigid constitutions** have tremendous difficulties in changing their written constitutions when change is needed.

> Rigid constitution: a constitution in which both the underlying principles, such as republicanism, and the ordinary rules, such as the powers of the prime minister, are very difficult to alter.

6 *The 2010 election manifestos — plans for the constitution*

Constitutional issues featured largely in all the major party manifestos (and those of the SNP, UKIP, the Greens and the BNP also had significant constitutional implications). The polls during the campaign suggested that there could be a hung (balanced) Parliament, which meant that the constitutional implications of minority or coalition government were much debated.

The main constitutional changes in the Labour Party's 2010 manifesto were:
- referendums on further reform of the Lords and changing the voting system
- voting at 16
- fixed-term Parliaments
- a register of lobbyists
- more powers devolved to local councils
- tighter regulation of MPs

The main constitutional changes in the Conservative Party's 2010 manifesto were:
- tighter regulation of MPs
- fewer MPs
- controls on party funding
- making it easier to petition Parliament and get it to debate issues
- devolution of power to local authorities and Scotland, Wales and Northern Ireland
- elimination of quangos
- restoration of civil liberties
- 'rolling back the state'

> Note the differences between the Conservatives and the Liberal Democrats, who formed a coalition government in 2010. Which party had to compromise most?

The main constitutional changes in the Liberal Democratic Party's manifesto were:
- proportional representation
- fixed-term Parliaments
- voting at 16
- an elected second chamber
- reform of party funding

- devolution of more power to local councils
- elected local police and health boards
- greater power for the House of Commons to regulate the executive
- a written constitution
- restoration of civil liberties

It is worth looking at what the parties promised in 1997 and 2010, and then noting how many of those changes to the constitution actually happened.

This is a central topic for all exam boards. You need to be very familiar with the powers and influence of the prime minister, and must have a good knowledge of cabinet and its role. The examiners will expect a good working knowledge of prime ministers from John Major onwards and at least outline knowledge of the impact that Margaret Thatcher had on the office and its powers. Lots of examples of what prime ministers have, or have not, been able to do need to be known to provide the essential facts to back up the points you make in your answers. There is a compulsory question on it for OCR.

To do well on this topic you need to:

- have a really good working knowledge of the work of John Major, Tony Blair and Gordon Brown, so that you have lots of examples to illustrate the work of the prime minister
- make sure you have a good 'textbook' knowledge of the theoretical roles

Short questions

1 What are the powers of the prime minister?
2 What is the role of the cabinet?
3 What are the limits to prime-ministerial power?
4 What is meant by collective responsibility?

Essay questions

5 Discuss the view that the prime minister has too much power.
6 To what extent has the UK prime minister become 'presidential'?
7 Does the cabinet still have an important role to play in the government of the UK?
8 How different was Gordon Brown's prime-ministerial 'style' from that of his predecessors?

Make sure you can back up your points with recent examples of the work of prime ministers.

1 *The evolution of the office of prime minister*

Like so many other parts of our unwritten constitution, the office of prime minister developed slowly over several centuries. By the end of the eighteenth century, largely as a result of the work of two men, Robert Walpole and William Pitt (who lived in Downing Street), the office had developed into something that we can recognise today.

By 1800, the prime minister:

- had control of all major appointments, not only of ministers and civil servants but also of key figures such as judges, generals and bishops
- was able to set the nation's agenda, deciding on policy, both domestic and foreign, as well as dominating Parliament and the law-making process
- needed to be able to dominate Parliament, and to have the support of the majority of the MPs there

- needed the ability to manage a team of ministers (the cabinet had also emerged by the end of the eighteenth century)
- had to be a good administrator, and to manage the economy and the country in times of crisis
- had to demonstrate leadership skills and the ability to communicate well

The key limitations were also there, such as the need for:
- party support
- the support of Parliament
- popular support

2 *The sources of prime-ministerial power*

Unlike the presidents of France or the USA, whose powers are listed in their country's constitution, the **powers** of the UK prime minister come from a variety of sources.

2.1 The old royal prerogatives

Prerogatives were the powers that our Medieval monarchs had, such as the ability to declare war, summon parliaments and appoint ministers. Over the centuries these powers were gradually transferred from monarchs to prime ministers. The prime minister now decides who heads the armed services and when troops should be withdrawn from Afghanistan.

2.2 Head of the executive

The prime minister exercises the role of head of the executive — the principal and final decision taker in the country. There is a general expectation that this person will provide leadership, initiate policies and broadly influence the direction in which the country is going. It was Gordon Brown who, when the banking system collapsed in 2008, took the key decisions on how to solve these problems. He would have been strongly criticised if he had failed to act, although there is no written rule that says that the prime minister has to act when bankers behave stupidly.

2.3 Head of a political party

This gives the prime minister tremendous influence over the making of policy through the party manifesto. If the prime minister's party has a majority in Parliament, the party leader (who is also prime minister) is able to put his ideas into practice by making them the law of the land. Tony Blair, who was Labour party leader in 1997, wished to see devolution for Scotland: that idea went into the Labour party manifesto. When Labour won that year's election with a large majority in Parliament, Scotland gained devolution. Many people vote for a party leader rather than for the party itself or its Parliamentary candidates. This enables prime ministers who have won elections to see it as the public approving of them individually and their policies, and gives them greater authority over their party.

Power: the ability to get things done, or make others do things they may not want to do. Gordon Brown had the 'power' to order the bailout of the banks in 2008.

Note that a formal list of the powers of the prime minister has never been drawn up.

Look at the role of Gordon Brown during the banking crisis of 2008–09.

2.4 Emergency powers

Not only are specific powers given to the prime minister in Emergency Powers Acts (1920, 1964) to enable him or her to act in an emergency of any type, but there is also an expectation on the part of the public that the prime minister will act decisively in an emergency. There can be a much greater willingness by the public during a crisis to accept that the prime minister needs more powers to solve problems, such as the terrorist threat after 9/11 and the London underground bombings, or the financial crisis of 2008–09.

3 *The role of the prime minister*

3.1 Key roles

Thee are several key roles which the prime minister is expected to fulfil.

Head of the executive

The prime minister is in charge of the whole administrative structure of the UK, ranging from local issues such as education through to the armed services and the defence of the UK. He or she can expect to be questioned, and held accountable for, every aspect of the work of the executive.

Policy maker

The prime minister is expected to be responsible for every aspect of national policy, ranging from healthcare to law and order.

Provider of vision and strategic direction

The prime minister is expected to provide a broad vision for the country's future, for example, that the UK should become much more 'European', as well as providing the broad strategy of how this might be achieved.

Party head

The prime minister is head of a political party and is expected to play a major role in making party policy and winning elections for the party.

Patronage

The prime minister is expected to play a lead role in appointing members of the Lords and Church of England bishops, and in the awarding of honours.

Parliament

The prime minister is seen as the 'leader' of Parliament and is expected to play a key role in participating in it.

Overseas

The prime minister is expected to meet and greet other nations' leaders, attend conferences such as the G7, and play a central role in making international policy on issues such as climate change and overseas aid.

Communicator

The prime minister is expected to be available to the public, the media and Parliament, not only to be questioned but also to communicate with everybody and explain what is happening and why.

Look carefully at the very high level of expectation placed on the prime minister.

Decision taker

The prime minister is expected to take all necessary decisions to ensure the smooth running and security of the UK.

3.2 Key powers

The prime minister has a number of key powers.

Appointment and dismissal of ministers

This is seen as the major power. The loyal and obedient can be rewarded, and opponents and rivals can be dismissed. The prime minister can put key supporters and those who agree with his or her views into key offices, such as chancellor of the exchequer. When he became prime minister, David Cameron's first task was to appoint his cabinet.

Appointment of cabinet committees

This is seen as a very important power as more and more policy decisions, such as constitutional reform, are dealt with by small groups of cabinet ministers. Who is on what committee is decided by the prime minister.

Other appointments

The prime minister also plays an important part in deciding other appointments, such as the heads of the armed services and the chair of governors of the BBC.

Control of the government agenda

Some issues, such as a financial crisis, will force themselves onto a government's agenda. However, the prime minister is able to assert his or her authority and give policies they favour real priority. Examples of this are:

- Thatcher on privatisation
- Major on the Citizen's Charter and European integration
- Blair on the Northern Ireland peace process, the economic ideas of New Labour and the invasion of Iraq
- Brown on public service reform

Control of the civil service

The prime minister plays a major role in the appointment of top civil servants. This means that not only the ministers heading departments but also the senior civil servants are loyal to the prime minister.

Control of Parliament

With a majority in Parliament the prime minister is able to ensure that his or her ideas become law. The prime minister appoints three key figures who have the responsibility of ensuring that his or her wishes go through Parliament:

- the leader of the House of Commons
- the leader of the House of Lords
- the government chief whip

Influence over the media

The prime minister is always in the news, and with the aid of his or her press secretary/spin doctor is able to play a large role in setting an agenda for the media. Tony Blair was very successful in using this influence, but Gordon Brown was less successful.

> To what extent are the powers of a prime minister limited in a coalition government?

Peerages and other honours

The prime minister controls the awarding of peerages and other honours, such as knighthoods, and can use this to reward loyal supporters. Both Gordon Brown and Tony Blair placed several long-term Labour supporters in the House of Lords.

3.3 Changes in powers

A variety of factors can lead to changes in a prime minster's powers including:

- good electoral performance: Tony Blair won three elections
- policy success or failures
- polls and the media turning against the prime minister
- varying influence over the cabinet
- varying support in the prime minister's parliamentary party
- the size of the government's majority in the Commons
- the personality of the prime minister
- the state of the economy
- patronage, particularly making poor use of it
- party divisions
- rivals
- electoral prospects
- the quality of the opposition
- coalition government

3.4 Limits to power

A number of factors can act to limit a prime minister's power, including:

- the attitude of their party — in the case of both Thatcher and Blair it was their party that played a key role in ending their career
- the availability of talent for the cabinet
- public opinion turning hostile
- the media, for example the role of the Murdoch press since 1990
- the cabinet, and the need to balance the cabinet with colleagues from all sections of the party
- the civil service, which can prove a restraining force, especially the Treasury
- the opposition — a well-led opposition can prove a serious obstacle
- Parliament — it has enormous powers over the prime minister, through instruments such as a motion of no confidence
- pressure groups
- coalition partners

Get your own examples of prime ministers having their authority checked.

4 *The prime minister's support team*

Traditionally the prime minister has been given a support team in No 10 to help him or her carry out the duties required of the post. This team consisted of:

- the Policy Unit
- the Political Office
- the Private Office
- the Press Office

David Cameron promised to reduce the size and influence of the staff at No 10.

A number of changes were made during Tony Blair's premiership, which centralised much more power in No 10. The number of people working directly for the prime minister went from the 100 under his predecessor John Major to more than 200. Blair exercised much more control over the Cabinet Office, and he had more special advisors. He gave more power to these advisors, in particular Jonathan Powell and Alastair Campbell: they could give orders to civil servants. A number of new bodies were created to support the prime minister:

- an unofficial 'prime minister's department'
- the Policy Directorate
- the Forward Strategy Unit
- the Delivery Unit
- the Foreign Policy Directorate
- the Public Sector Reform Unit
- the Communications and Strategy Unit
- the Directorate of Government Relations

5 *Prime-ministerial styles*

5.1 Recent prime ministers

Recent prime ministers have had quite different styles.

Gordon Brown
- Seen as a 'principled pragmatist'.
- Totally committed to the job and objectives.
- A poor communicator.
- Authoritarian — described as 'Stalinist'.
- Reluctant to delegate to an Alastair Campbell or Jonathan Powell — tendency to try to 'micromanage'.
- Gave a limited role to the cabinet and its members.
- Ran less of the 'sofa' government of Tony Blair — was more directive.
- Less inclined to consult others.
- Favoured 'GOATS': 'Government of All the Talents' — tried bringing outsiders such as Digby Jones and Alan Sugar into government.
- Brought many of his former Treasury civil servants into No 10.
- Liked working with his own small team.

To what extent has David Cameron developed a different style from Gordon Brown?

Tony Blair
- A strong communicator who placed tremendous importance on getting his message across.
- Pushed his middle-class, 'ordinary', 'regular-guy' image.
- Used informal 'sofa government' methods.
- Very 'media savvy'.
- Spent less time in Parliament than his predecessors.
- Made less use of the cabinet and civil service than predecessors, and more use of his own political advisors.
- Good at apologising for his mistakes.
- Had very strong convictions and personal beliefs.
- Liked being a war and world leader.

- Played a dominant role in his administration.
- Hennessy refers to it as a 'command premiership'.

John Major
- Collegial — preferred to try to work with a team.
- Listened to his party — unlike his predecessor, Thatcher.
- Proved to be weaker in power than Thatcher and Blair, particularly as he had a small majority and a divided party.
- Used the cabinet more and aimed at attaining a consensus.
- Tended to be indecisive.
- Allowed ministers to dominate policy, e.g. Kenneth Clarke at the Treasury.
- Aimed at stability rather than radical change.

Margaret Thatcher
- Forceful — prepared to be ruthless when it came to sacking ministers.
- Radical and visionary, a real 'conviction' politician.
- Success in three elections in a row.
- Abrasive, dominant and ruthless.

6 *The debate on styles of government*

Different prime ministers can have different approaches to government. Here some of the characteristics of three styles of government.

6.1 Cabinet government

The traditional picture of the UK having cabinet government is now dead (if it ever existed).
- The prime minister was supposed to be *primus inter pares* — merely the first among equals.
- Strategy was decided by the cabinet.
- Key decisions and policy were decided by the cabinet.
- The cabinet was the focal point of the government.

6.2 Prime-ministerial government

- The prime minister dominates the media and is the spokesperson for the government.
- The prime minister rarely attends the House of Commons and sees Parliament as of limited importance.
- The cabinet is downgraded in status and meets less often, and is less involved in decision making.
- Key civil service appointments are made by No 10.
- The prime minister works more with his or her own people and less with ministers and civil servants.
- The prime minister dominates the policy-making process.
- The prime minister checks all major decisions taken by ministers — 'micromanages'.

Make sure you have a clear picture in your own mind of what you mean by prime-ministerial government as opposed to presidential government.

- The prime minister dominates foreign policy and makes the key decisions regarding the EU.
- The personality of the prime minister is vital to the whole administration.

6.3 Presidential government

'Presidential' system: the system whereby the president is both the head of state (the monarch in the UK) and head of the executive, and has both more powers and fewer limits to those powers than the 'conventional' prime minister has.

Be careful about seeing the UK prime minister as '**presidential**' and just assuming that presidents are all-powerful. US presidents are limited by a written constitution in which:
- their cabinet appointments have to be vetted by Congress
- they have limited influence over legislation
- broad areas of national life such as education, crime and punishment are not under their jurisdiction
- they have limited control over the economy
- they are under major restrictions in foreign policy

A better example might be the French president, who:
- is directly elected
- appoints the prime minister and assists the prime minister with other key appointments
- chairs the council of ministers (cabinet)
- has a veto over legislation
- decides on holding referendums
- can dissolve Parliament
- makes key appointments in the civil service and armed forces
- controls all key foreign policy, defence and EU issues
- plays a key role in the management of the economy
- is subject to less accountability — does not face the equivalent of Prime Minister's Question Time

6.4 Possible reforms

To what extent has David Cameron changed the office of prime minister?

A number of reforms to the office of prime minister have been considered, including:
- creating a proper prime minister's department which is both transparent and accountable
- reducing the royal prerogatives the prime minister controls, such as going to war
- establishing a formal and recognised role for the cabinet in the decision-making process
- requiring parliamentary consent for major decisions, such as going to war

7 *The cabinet*

7.1 The evolution of the cabinet

- The cabinet system first developed in the eighteenth century.
- By 1800 the cabinet consisted of the prime minister and key ministers.
- All members of the cabinet were in the Lords or Commons.
- It was accountable to Parliament.

- It was where key decisions were taken.
- It was collectively responsible for decisions taken.

7.2 The role of cabinet today

- It is the central clearing house for decisions which may be taken elsewhere.
- It is vital for the coordination of government.
- The cabinet is the place where policies are endorsed by all members of the government.
- It is responsible for crisis management.
- It sets the agenda for Parliament.
- It can act as a brake on the prime minister or a radical minister.
- It referees disputes between departments.
- It provides a vital link between party, Parliament, the legal system and government. It joins all parts of the system of government together.
- Thatcher, Blair and Brown have all been criticised for downgrading the status and role of the cabinet.
- It is sometimes at risk of becoming too large for effective decision taking.

Analyse how a coalition government has changed the role of the cabinet.

A Labour cabinet member said, on resigning in 2003, 'There is no real collective responsibility because there is no collective, just diktats in favour of increasingly badly thought through initiatives that come from on high'.

7.3 Composition of the cabinet

The composition of the cabinet:

- is subject to the decision of the prime minister
- is usually 20 or more people
- includes key ministers, such as defence, chancellor, foreign secretary
- may include a smaller 'inner', 'kitchen', or 'war' cabinet, depending on the wishes of the prime minister
- usually includes two or three members of the House of Lords — the rest are MPs

How has a coalition government changed the composition of the cabinet?

7.4 Cabinet committees

Cabinet committees are appointed by the prime minister to deal with specific areas of government or issues, such as the economy. They:

- are smaller than main cabinet, usually consisting of seven to nine ministers
- can include non-cabinet ministers
- include standing cabinet committees for areas such as domestic affairs and national security
- may be appointed on an 'ad hoc' basis to deal with issues such as pandemic influenza planning or climate change
- have played a smaller role since Thatcher
- may make recommendations for the Queen's Speech (legislation), deal with long-term strategic planning, or be set up to manage specific crises
- are serviced by the Cabinet Office and the cabinet secretary

TOPIC 7

The prime minister and cabinet

Collective responsibility: a convention (a custom which has the force of law) which applies to all members of the cabinet in the UK. It says that once a decision has been taken by a member of the cabinet, or by the cabinet as a whole, individual members of the cabinet must support that decision in public, or resign.

7.5 Collective responsibility

When appointed as a member of the government, a minister has to accept the principle of **collective responsibility**:

- It is a long-established convention.
- It requires the minister to treat all cabinet business as confidential (and not to leak it to the press!).
- It requires the minister to support all other ministers and their policies in public, even though they may disagree with the policy.
- It requires the minister to resign if they feel they cannot support any government policy.
- Its purpose is to provide all ministers with the full support of all the other members of the government and to ensure at least the appearance of unity in a government.
- It applies to all members of the government — but particularly to cabinet.
- The best examples of resignations over collective responsibility were those of Short and Cook in 2003 over the Iraq war.
- Tony Blair and Gordon Brown were both very firm on insisting on it.
- Critics of the convention argue that it is wrong for ministers to have to defend policies they do not agree with and may have had no part in planning.

8 The prime minister and cabinet in a coalition government

The election of 2010, which gave no single party an overall majority in the House of Commons, led to the formation of a coalition government. This had a major impact on both the prime minister and the cabinet, not least because the new prime minister, Conservative Party leader David Cameron, was obliged to include a number of Liberal Democrats as ministers in his cabinet, with their leader Nick Clegg as deputy prime minister. The prime minister's freedom in government was reduced, as:

- he had no overall majority in the House of Commons, which was likely to give backbenchers of both parties in the coalition more influence
- he had to consult his Liberal Democratic partners on all major policy issues
- key departments had ministers from different parties, for example the Treasury, with a Conservative chancellor and a Liberal Democratic Chief Secretary, which would make decision taking more difficult

The cabinet's status was likely to rise as a coordinating body responsible for ensuring that the two parties in government managed to 'sing from the same hymn sheet'. The new arrangement would, however, put the convention of collective responsibility under stress, as members of one party in the government would have to publicly support policies which they had clearly opposed in their manifestos.

The prime minister was able to impose some of his own wishes on the new government, for example in creating the new National Security Council and deciding on its membership and role, and in reducing the number of policy advisers in No 10 and in the government generally.

Ministers and the civil service

All three boards have similar requirements for this topic. Knowledge and understanding of the work of ministers and the importance of ministerial responsibility is essential. Detailed knowledge of the civil service is not required; the focus is on ministers, ministerial responsibility, and, for AQA and OCR, the relationship between ministers and senior civil servants.

To do well in this topic you need to :

- have a good picture of the different roles and responsibilities of ministers and civil servants
- be able to define ministerial responsibility (as opposed to collective responsibility) and give relevant examples of it in operation

Short questions

1 What is meant by ministerial responsibility?
2 Describe the relationship between ministers and senior civil servants.
3 Describe the difference between a government department, an agency and a quango.
4 What is the role of a minister?

Essay questions

5 Discuss the importance of the convention of ministerial responsibility.
6 Discuss the view that civil servants should have more power.

> Do not confuse ministers with MPs.

1 The different types of government minister

1.1 Cabinet ministers

Cabinet ministers are the heads of the major departments of state. A good example of a cabinet minister is the foreign secretary, who will be expected to:

- take responsibility for, and manage, the conduct of foreign policy
- do further cabinet work, sit on key cabinet committees and share responsibility for the whole conduct of government policy
- answer questions in Parliament and appear before select committees of the House of Commons dealing with his or her department's work
- ensure that any legislation covering foreign affairs passes through Parliament
- travel widely and visit other countries and the UN
- be involved in political party work, as a senior member of a political party
- spend time dealing with constituency matters, as an elected MP
- attend the House of Commons and vote on key bills

There is some debate as to whether cabinet ministers have too many roles and are not able to perform them all properly. However, cabinet ministers do receive a substantial additional salary over and above what they get as MPs.

You might consider their workload and responsibilities. Is it reasonable to ask so much of one individual? Can the UK be well served by people who have so much to do? Perhaps the Americans have the right idea when they forbid anyone from being both a minister and a member of their parliament (Congress). This is known as the separation of powers, which means that a person is not allowed to be both a member of the legislature and a member of the executive.

1.2 Ministers of state/junior ministers

There are usually about 70 junior ministers. One or two of them will be allocated to major departments such as the Foreign Office to assist the foreign secretary. They will be given specific areas of responsibility under the cabinet minister: for example, a 'minister for Europe', who has a particular responsibility for the relationship between the UK and the EU. The minister for Europe will report both to the foreign secretary and to the prime minister. Ministers of state get an additional salary and may well be expected to answer questions in Parliament and help get legislation through. About 20% of junior ministers may progress into the cabinet, but for the majority this is as high up the promotion ladder as they will go.

Not all ministers are in the cabinet, but all are bound by collective responsibility, even in a coalition government.

When the cabinet is included, the total number of ministers — those paid salaries in addition to their pay as an MP — is about 100. A few will be members of the House of Lords.

2 Ministerial responsibility

Ministerial responsibility is a vital part of the whole democratic process, as it is through this process that citizens and taxpayers can call those who take decisions on their behalf to account. It means that a minister is accountable for all that happens in his or her area of responsibility.

For example, the secretary of state for defence is responsible for all matters concerning the defence of the UK. If the RAF proves to be incompetent in a war, then it is the minister's responsibility to take the blame for this, find out what happened, discipline those who have failed and take steps to ensure that it does not happen again. The minister will have to explain this to Parliament, the media, cabinet colleagues and the prime minister.

If there is clear evidence that the minister has been incompetent or made a major error of judgement, then he or she must resign. Lord Carrington, foreign secretary in 1982, resigned over his failure to foresee the Argentinian invasion of the Falklands.

2.1 Types of ministerial responsibility

There are two main types of ministerial responsibility:

Role responsibility

This is the responsibility ministers have for their department, for getting necessary laws through, for making necessary policy and for the general management of their department. When a major error of judgement or serious mismanagement occurs, resignation is expected:

- In 1992 the economy suffered a major reverse over the exchange rate mechanism and interest rates soared. The chancellor of the exchequer, Norman Lamont, eventually resigned.
- Estelle Morris, the Labour education secretary, resigned in 2002 over the major problems caused by the introduction of the new A-level examination.
- Beverley Hughes, a Home Office minister, had to resign in 2004 over mistakes she made in UK immigration policy.
- David Laws, chief secretary to the Treasury, resigned in 2010 over his expenses claims.

Personal responsibility

This means that ministers have to take responsibility for their own personal conduct. If they break the law or indulge in behaviour that the public, the media and the prime minister do not approve of, then they have to resign. In 1998 the secretary of state for Wales resigned over what he called a 'moment of madness' on Clapham Common. In the same year the secretary of state for trade and industry, Peter Mandelson, was forced to resign when it was revealed that he had 'forgotten' to declare that he had been lent a large sum of money by Geoffrey Robinson, another minister, whose business dealings Mandelson's department was investigating. Peter Mandelson was brought back into the cabinet as secretary of state for Northern Ireland, but had to resign again when questions were raised in the media about allegations of assistance to Indian citizens who desired UK passports and who had also donated money to the Millennium Dome project.

Other examples arising from the MPs' expenses scandal are Hazel Blears and Shahid Malik, both ministers who resigned.

A coalition government, where a department might have ministers from different parties in it, will place additional strain on ministerial responsibility.

2.2 Flaws in ministerial responsibility

The main failing with the principle is that it does not always seem to work. In the case of the BSE disaster, blame could not be allotted until long after the relevant ministers had left office and the civil servants had retired or moved to other responsibilities.

If the minister retains the support of the prime minister, as in the case of William Waldegrave over the sale of arms to Iraq in 1989–90, nothing happens. In the case of alleged salmonella in eggs, it was the junior minister Edwina Currie (not the cabinet minister) who was forced to resign after a sustained campaign by Tory backbenchers and the National Farmers' Union demanding a scapegoat.

The convention (an unwritten rule that has the force of a law) is fine in theory. The public ought to know who must shoulder the responsibility for mistakes. However, it seems to vary in practice. An important example is the case of the former home secretary Michael Howard. In 1995 there were some serious escapes by major criminals from prisons in the UK. Prisons are the responsibility of the home secretary, but Howard did not resign. Instead he sacked the head of the Prison Service, maintaining that it was his fault. But in 1998, long after Michael Howard had left office, it was discovered that he had failed to provide Parliament with information, which if known at the time, might have resulted in his being forced to resign. With more and more decisions being taken by unelected quangos and heads of agencies, responsibility can be difficult to allocate.

The Scott Report of 1996 condemned several ministers for their conduct in the sale of arms to Iraq. This had been done in secret and in clear breach of official policy, which had been approved by Parliament. In the end the prime minister, John Major, did not require any of them to resign, and in fact some of the relevant ministers and civil servants were promoted. However, the resignation of Stephen Byers (transport minister) in 2002, for the perceived failure of several of his transport policies, reinforced the convention.

There is a growing feeling that the convention of ministerial responsibility lacks real 'teeth'. But if the media put on enough pressure, or raise sufficient public indignation over an issue, then the prime minister will stop trying to 'ride it out' and require resignation. When a prime minister asks a minister to resign, it is convention always to obey.

3 The development of the civil service

3.1 Origins of the civil service

All monarchs needed help to administer the nation and collect taxes, so Britain always had a group of officials who served the state. By the middle of the nineteenth century it was becoming very clear that those who helped ministers to run the day-to-day business of their departments were simply not up to the job. When Britain went to war with Russia in the Crimea (1854–56), many thousands of soldiers died because of the incompetence of the support and supply services: in other words, the civil servants who helped administer the army and navy. A sustained press campaign, which pointed out their incompetence, led to major changes.

3.2 Changes in the mid-nineteenth century

Two men, Northolt and Trevelyan, led the inquiry into the civil service following the Crimean War. It recommended that in future civil servants be appointed not because they happened to be related to an important political figure, but on grounds of merit alone. The inquiry's main recommendations were as follows:
- Civil servants should be promoted on merit.
- Civil servants should be recruited through a tough competitive exam.
- The examination should be in the liberal arts.
- Men with technical expertise or experience in other walks of life were not welcome.

The aim was to obtain a small highly educated elite to advise ministers on policy. Although these men may not have been experts in economics or defence, it was assumed that they were intelligent enough to acquire the necessary expertise.

3.3 Twentieth-century developments in the civil service

The intention of Gladstone, Northcote and Trevelyan was that an elected minister, chosen by the people and accountable to Parliament, should be advised by a small elite group of civil servants on matters of policy. Once a policy had been decided by a minister after discussion with senior civil servants (e.g. to change the system of taxation) and Parliament had approved it, then it

would be handed over to more junior civil servants to carry out. The minister and Parliament would ensure that the civil servants did the job properly.

However, the civil service grew rapidly in size, from a few thousand to more than 750,000 men and women in the course of the twentieth century. The main reason for this was that the state took on more and more tasks which had to be administered, ranging from housing and education to roads and health. Huge numbers of civil servants were needed to manage all these tasks.

You do not need to know the detailed structure of the civil service — just make sure you are aware of its main roles and responsibilities.

3.4 Concerns in the late twentieth century

From the middle of the twentieth century onwards, there were growing concerns about the civil service. They were as follows:

- It was not giving good advice to ministers. Civil servants were felt to be conservative and out of touch with contemporary needs.
- It had taken on tasks — such as running the telephone system — which it was unfit to do. There was a real lack of managerial expertise in the civil service.
- It had become far too big and expensive. Simply paying and providing office space for three-quarters of a million men and women was a huge drain on public spending.
- It was recruiting the wrong sort of individual. Selecting arts graduates from Oxford and Cambridge was not providing ministers with the informed and expert advice they needed.
- It was spending its time administering departments and not advising ministers on what might be the best policy options. Its role had changed from what had been intended.
- It was making too many mistakes — look up the Crichel Down affair and the spy scandal over Burgess and Maclean.
- It was not properly accountable — it was too vast for ministers to control and the public could not find out information about it.
- It was preventing the radical reform needed to deal with the UK's economy and social problems.
- It was reluctant to retrain to adapt to new tasks, and hostile to new ideas about how to carry out its tasks.
- It lacked technical skills and was hostile to experts.
- It lacked the management skills needed to run major departments that had thousands of employees.

Margaret Thatcher was very unhappy about the support she had received from her civil servants when she was a minister between 1970 and 1974. When she came to power in 1979 she was determined to change the civil service — and she did.

3.5 The Thatcher reforms

Margaret Thatcher (prime minister 1979–90) introduced a series of reforms that changed the civil service as radically as Gladstone's had a century before. Although she was opposed by the Labour opposition at the time, the Blair/Brown governments did not reverse her reforms.

Thatcher made huge changes to the civil service, as she did in so many other areas of government.

These were the key ones:

- The civil service was reduced in size from about 750,000 in 1979 to fewer than 500,000 when Thatcher left office.
- The Civil Service Department, which the prime minister felt was too 'soft' on civil service pay and conditions, was abolished. Control over the civil service was given to the Treasury, which took a much more hardline view on pay, promotion and conditions of service.
- Performance-related pay was introduced and the government started to reduce the job security that civil servants had enjoyed.
- An Efficiency Unit was set up under an outside businessman, Derek Rayner, to reduce costs. It led to millions of pounds of savings, but not quite the billions Thatcher had hoped for.
- The Financial Management Initiative was instituted. The aim was to bring much more efficient management practices, such as clear target setting, into the civil service. It was hoped to encourage initiative, end bureaucracy and introduce more expertise.
- Privatisation and market testing were introduced. Some functions that had always been performed by the civil service, such as developing software for civil service computers, were contracted out to private companies. There had been a Department for Energy, but as gas and electricity utilities were sold off, these departments were no longer needed. Market testing required civil servants to compete with outsiders for their jobs.
- Margaret Thatcher took care to interview candidates for the top posts in the civil service. In the past, ministers had tended to accept the advice of their civil servants. Thatcher insisted on interviewing them personally, and frequently rejected her civil servants' advice. She was looking for more radical men and women who were prepared to show commitment to her aims and objectives. This led to the famous quote 'Is he one of us?' — in other words, did the person in question support her radical agenda?

These reforms all had some effect, but by 1987 it was felt that the civil service still required further reform. As a result, Thatcher asked a prominent businessman, Robin Ibbs, to report on the civil service.

The Ibbs Report — the 'Next Steps' programme

When Ibbs examined the civil service, he found that it was too big, it lacked innovative talent, it failed to provide the taxpayer with value for money, it placed too little focus on quality advice for ministers, and it spent too much time administering things inefficiently. He made the following recommendations:

- The administrative functions of the civil service, such as dealing with driving licences and collecting taxes, should be handed over to agencies. These should be separate from ordinary civil service/government departments such as the Foreign Office. These new agencies would specialise in one particular area, such as prisons or immigration.
- Ninety-five per cent of civil servants should work in agencies, taking their broad instructions from ministers (e.g. toughening up the driving test) and then using their own managerial skills to administer that policy properly.
- Only a few of the 'traditional' civil servants should remain in London and other cities, advising ministers on policy. They would form about 5% of

the total and focus on policy advice. It was hoped that they would be more innovative and radical than their predecessors, and not be weighed down by administering vast departments.

Margaret Thatcher left office in 1990, before being able to carry out these ideas, but John Major (1990–97) did.

3.6 Civil service reforms under John Major, 1990–97

By 1998, 124 agencies had been set up, such as the Prison Agency which was to run prisons under the broad instructions of the home secretary. These agencies employed nearly 75% of all civil servants. Some agencies are huge, such as the Benefits Agency which employs over 70,000 people; others, such as the Royal Mint, have only a few hundred. Tony Blair's government continued the programme. This included further privatisation, such as that of Department of Social Security property.

Although ridiculed at the time, partly for its famous 'cones hotline', John Major's idea for a Citizen's Charter was sound and it became firmly established. The aim was to ensure that citizens received better service from civil servants, particularly those agencies and departments that came into contact with the public, such as the Passport Office and employment centres.

Each agency had to publish performance targets. The results they achieved were to be published, and also there had to be a clear and known way for the public to complain about poor service and receive compensation. There was to be a real focus in departments and agencies on serving the public well. It was hoped that they would be both 'civil' to and good 'servants' of the public.

Service First

This was largely the same as the Citizen's Charter, but was the name given to it by the Blair government of 1997–2001, possibly because Labour had been so critical of the Citizen's Charter when in opposition. A small team in the Cabinet Office ran it, and they put a lot of pressure on departments and agencies to respond quickly to public queries and concerns.

3.7 Civil service change under Tony Blair and Gordon Brown

In spite of much criticism of Conservative changes, Labour continued with most, and even accelerated those changes. This included:
- expanding the agency programme
- more target setting for civil servants
- performance-related pay
- market testing of new services
- contracting out of public service provision
- selling off state-owned assets, such as government offices
- more special advisors for ministers from outside the civil service
- the 'Service First' programme, designed to improve the quality of service to the public
- expanding the freedom of information idea

These changes are a good example of prime-ministerial power.

New Labour proved to be very similar to 'Thatcherism' in many respects.

In February 2005 Tony Blair gave a major speech on what he hoped to achieve with the civil service in the future. He argued for:

- a much smaller 'strategic' group working with ministers in London
- employing more civil servants with specialist skills — less amateurism
- having a civil service more accessible to the public generally, and using the private and voluntary sectors much more to deliver services to the public
- more rapid promotion within the civil service for the able — fixed-term contracts for those at the top
- much more focus on developing leadership and strategic management skills
- a much more strategic and innovative approach to policy making

In other words, Blair was arguably continuing the ideas of Margaret Thatcher.

3.8 Monitoring of the civil service

The main ways in which the civil service is monitored and taxpayers can ensure they get value for money are as follows:

- The minister is always in charge and has the final say over appointments, conduct and policy. The minister is almost invariably an elected MP (although a few might be members of the House of Lords) and therefore 'represents' the democratic process.
- People have rights of complaint and redress under the Citizen's Charter.
- People can complain to the ombudsman (the parliamentary commissioner for administration), who can investigate some complaints and publicise incompetence by the civil service.
- Select committees of the House of Commons are empowered to question civil servants.
- When civil servants break the law — for example, by taking bribes — they can, of course, be prosecuted.
- MPs can question ministers in Parliament about civil servants' conduct.
- The Public Accounts Committee of the House of Commons can monitor a department's expenditure.
- The media can highlight incompetence or failure.

Make sure you know the ways in which the civil service can be called to account.

3.9 The role of the higher civil servant

The primary role of senior civil servants is to advise ministers. It is their job to give ministers the information they want and need, and to advise them impartially to the best of their ability. They should warn ministers of the consequences of their actions. Once the minister has made a decision, however, it is the job of civil servants to carry out that task, whether they agree with it or not. Civil servants should remain anonymous, impartial and neutral when carrying out their duties. They must not divulge any information about their work unless ordered to do so by their minister.

Clearly there can be major difficulties in the relationship between ministers and their civil servants. Democracy requires that the civil servant carries out the wishes of the democratically elected minister. However, if the minister, who might be both ignorant and wrong, insists on a policy that an able and experienced civil servant knows will harm citizens, then what should the civil servant do?

3.10 The impact of the Conservative reforms

The civil service is now smaller and cheaper, and certainly more efficient, than it was before 1979. On the other hand, concerns have sometimes been voiced that the civil service is too 'politicised' — that it worries too much about appealing to its current political masters and not about giving ministers the best advice, or protecting the public from the incompetence of ministers. There is also concern that it is difficult for ministers, and thus the public, to control the new agencies, and that democracy has suffered as a result.

4 *The non-civil service*

4.1 The growth of political advisors

An important development under Margaret Thatcher, which was continued by Tony Blair and Gordon Brown, is the appointment of political advisors. In the past, ministers took their advice almost entirely from established and experienced civil servants. Now all senior ministers can appoint political advisors. These advisors can come from many different backgrounds and are given a salary similar to that of a senior civil servant. Their job is to offer advice to the minister on topics of the minister's choice, and they have access to all the information in a department. Their position may be resented by the established and experienced civil servants.

> David Cameron's government has insisted on a reduction in the number of political advisors, both in No 10 and for individual ministers.

4.2 Quangos

'Quango' stands for quasi-autonomous non-governmental organisation. Quangos are groups of people who are not civil servants or local government officers, who are given responsibility for a particular public task. The members of a quango are appointed by the relevant minister, are accountable to that minister, are paid, and may work in either a full-time or a part-time capacity.

Here are some typical functions performed by quangos:
- Recommending to the secretary of state for education how much money should go to each university. The quango would also lay down the criteria by which universities get public money. Another quango inspects universities and publishes the university 'league tables'.
- Monitoring the examination boards. The secretary of state for education asked the head of QCDA (the quango monitoring all public exams) for a report in the summer of 2001 on the new AS exams and how to improve them. The secretary of state did not ask the inspectors from her own department.
- Monitoring new drugs before they are used on the public.
- Running hospitals.
- Regulating the privatised industries, such as electricity.

The role of quangos can be:
- executive, in that they have the power to act (e.g. to run prisons)
- advisory, in that they can recommend actions to the minister (e.g. to reduce the number of exams at AS)
- regulatory, in that they can agree, or forbid, activities in certain industries (e.g. regulating price rises in privatised industries such as telecommunications)

> The Conservative manifesto of 2010 pledged to reduce the number of quangos.

Disadvantages of quangos

There are several criticisms of quangos:

- Their members are not elected and are only accountable to a minister.
- They control huge amounts of public money (probably about 40% of public spending now).
- Ministers make appointments, and ministers are accused of giving well-paid jobs to their friends and supporters.
- It can be difficult for the public to find out information about them, although the Freedom of Information Act has made it easier.
- There is no real link between the tax-paying public and the quangos, which spend a lot of their money. It is argued that this is not right in a democracy.

Advantages of quangos

The number of quangos has grown steadily over the past 30 years. Their main merits are seen to be as follows:

- Experts can be used on a quango.
- Controversial issues, such as race relations and the content of school curricula, can be dealt with by impartial and independent experts, and removed from politics.
- Quangos tend to be quicker and cheaper than using civil servants and local government officials.
- Ministers can put their own supporters on a quango and rely on them to carry out the government's wishes. In contrast, civil servants or local authorities might slow down or obstruct government wishes.
- In enabling an elected government to achieve its objectives and manifesto promises, it could be argued that quangos are an aid to democracy.
- The head of a quango can be asked to resign to shield a minister from taking responsibility — as the resignation of Stubbs (head of QCA) over the 2002 A-level results demonstrated in 2002.

Parliament, the House of Commons and the House of Lords

This is a compulsory topic for all boards. OCR has a compulsory question on it. It has to be known in detail, and great care must be taken to ensure that you are fully up to date with developments in both Houses of Parliament. If asked a question about 'Parliament', remember that you must deal with both the House of Commons and the House of Lords, but if asked a question about the Commons specifically, then just mention the Commons and don't feel the need to discuss the Lords.

To do well in this topic you need to:

- make full use of the Parliament Channel on the television, as this will give you excellent examples of both Houses at work
- have a through and accurate knowledge of how Parliament actually works and what its role is

Short questions

1 Describe the work of the committees of the House of Commons.
2 Explain the role of the opposition in Parliament.
3 What are the powers of the House of Lords?
4 What are the main ways in which the House of Commons checks the executive?

Essay questions

5 How successfully does Parliament scrutinise the executive?
6 How well does the House of Commons perform its functions?
7 Discuss the view that the House of Lords should be abolished.
8 To what extent is Parliament a genuinely representative institution?

1 The development of Parliament

1.1 Parliament to 1600

There is evidence of a type of parliament, where the monarch consulted with his principal subjects on matters of great national importance, before the Norman Conquest of 1066. By 1500 the monarch was meeting regularly with two separate Houses of Parliament and gaining their consent for major issues such as taxation. The 'upper' House was made up of the hereditary peerage and the senior clergy, while the 'lower' House of Commons was made up of elected men, usually two from each major town or city and two from each county.

It is worth noting that the Tudor monarchs ensured that all the major laws changing the religion of England were passed through Parliament. By the end of the sixteenth century it was well established and accepted by all that a law which the king put forward, and which was supported by both Houses of Parliament, was superior to all other forms of law, and had to be obeyed even by the monarch.

1.2 Parliament from 1600 to the present

Two main features stand out in the development of Parliament in this period:

- the gradual supremacy that Parliament gained over the monarch
- the supremacy that the executive gained over Parliament

By 1850 the monarch had to sign bills that she or he did not like, had to create peers to get bills through the House of Lords and had to accept the prime minister and cabinet that Parliament and the electorate had chosen.

The twentieth century saw the government, provided it had a majority in the House of Commons, controlling most of what Parliament debated and legislated.

2 *The House of Commons*

2.1 Functions of the House of Commons

Legislation

A key function of the Commons is to make laws, which are binding on everyone in the UK. This might be a law that imposes speed limits on cars, changes the rules about immigration, or devolves power to a Scottish Parliament.

Executive scrutiny

The Commons has been entrusted with the key role of checking the actions of the government and all state employees, such as civil servants, and ensuring the vital principle of **accountability**. MPs have the power to dismiss governments or ministers, and to make them explain their actions.

Representation

Each MP comes from a specific part of the country, called a constituency (usually made up of about 75,000+ voters). MPs must look after the interests of the individuals in that constituency and the area in general, and speak up in Parliament on their behalf. MPs also represent the party of which they are a member, and may also represent other groups, such as trade unions or farmers, who give them financial backing.

Debate

We expect the House of Commons to debate the great issues of the day, be it policy towards Afghanistan or the future of genetic engineering. We expect the government of the day to listen to the ideas put forward by our representatives, and to have our own understanding of these issues enhanced by this public debate. Note the comparatively new 'Westminster Hall' debates, which give MPs more chance to debate major issues.

To provide ministers

Almost all UK ministers, including the prime minister, come from the House of Commons. Unlike in the USA, where there is a **separation of powers** and you cannot be a member of both the legislature and the executive, in the UK all ministers have to be members of Parliament. Whether it is right for the House of Commons both to provide ministers and then to try to check them is an important issue.

Accountability: the requirement for representatives to be answerable to their constituents for their behaviour and decisions.

Make sure you know the full range of MP's functions and can prioritise them.

Separation of powers: a system whereby the three parts of government — the executive, legislature and judiciary — are quite separate and it is not possible for one person to be a member of more than one part.

Legitimisation

Not only to give assent to all laws and taxes, but to support the government of the day in all its actions.

2.2 The powers of the House of Commons

In theory the House of Commons has enormous power, but in practice many of these powers are rarely used. They are:

- to reject or amend totally any bill put forward by a government
- to deny the government the money it needs to administer the country, or any specific policy — in other words to reject or amend the budget
- to dismiss a government or any member of the executive
- to use their law making or control-of-money powers to impose or prevent any policy they wish
- to summon and require answers from any citizen

The limited use made of most, if not all, of these powers is indicative of how much power has been transferred to the executive in the UK.

2.3 Members of the House of Commons

Party	University	Public school	Women	Over 40	Professional	Business	Miscellaneous	Manual	Ethnic
Labour	64%	18%	28%	71%	40%	13%	43%	10%	4%
Conservative	81%	60%	9%	65%	39%	38%	23%	1%	1%
Liberal Democratic	79%	39%	16%	60%	40%	29%	29%	2%	2%

Table 8.1 MPs elected in 2005

> Learn these statistics so you can deal with a question on how 'representative' our MPs are.

The MPs elected in 2010 had two significant characteristics. The first was the high proportion of new MPs (more than 30%) and the second was the decrease in the number of those with an education/public sector background and the increase in those with a finance/business/consultant background.

Public school	Oxbridge	University graduates	Women	Asian	Black	60+	40–59	Under 39
35%	30%	90%	21%	2.6%	1.4%	18%	63%	19%

Table 8.2 MPs elected in 2010

2.4 The role of backbenchers in the House of Commons

Most MPs are backbenchers. The simplest definition of a backbench MP is one who is not allowed to sit on the two front benches, directly in front of the speaker in the House of Commons. Backbenchers are the MPs of all parties who are not:

- cabinet ministers
- members of the government
- members of the shadow cabinet
- part of the opposition's front-bench team

Delegates and representatives: it is one of the traditional, but unwritten, rules that UK MPs are representatives and not delegates. A representative is chosen by a constituency to go to Westminster and take decisions on behalf of the constituency. An MP is expected to listen to constituents but still exercise his or her own judgement on, for example, a vote. If a local referendum were 100% in favour of legalising cannabis, a 'representative' MP would still be justified to vote against such a measure in Parliament if they felt it was the right decision.

To what extent has the role of the backbencher changed when there is a 'hung' Parliament?

An MP is now paid substantially less than a GP — do you think this is right?

It is important to differentiate between the roles of backbenchers from the government party and those from the opposition parties. Backbenchers from the government party are expected not to criticise the government too strongly, even when the interests of their constituents or constituency are at issue. Opposition backbenchers are expected to play a prominent part in opposing the government as well as looking after the interests of their constituency. Be aware of the debate about whether an MP should be a party **delegate** (and bound by party instructions) or a **representative** from his or her constituency. Representatives are supposed to be free agents who can judge each issue on its merits.

The main opportunities for backbenchers to represent their constituency and constituents in the House of Commons are as follows:

- Each parliamentary day usually opens with questions, which gives backbenchers of all parties the chance to question ministers.
- Backbenchers have the right to ask for a written answer to any question, and that answer is published in *Hansard* (the official record). These are probably of more value than oral questions.
- Backbenchers have the right to participate in all debates on legislation.
- Backbenchers have the right to vote on all bills.
- Each parliamentary day ends with an adjournment debate, when a backbencher has the opportunity to debate an issue that affects his or her constituency with the relevant minister, who has to be present and respond to the backbencher.
- All the main parliamentary committees, such as the general or public bill committees on bills and the select departmental committees, as well as the key scrutiny committee, the Public Accounts Committee, are chaired by backbenchers and the whole of their membership is made up of backbenchers.
- Backbenchers can refer matters dealing with possible maladministration to the ombudsman.
- Backbenchers have the right to raise any matter affecting a constituency with any minister, in writing, and they are guaranteed a reply.
- Backbenchers have the opportunity to put forward bills, known as Private Members' Bills, if they are successful in a ballot.
- Backbenchers can participate in, and control the agenda of, the debates in Westminster Hall.

The pay and conditions of backbenchers

- The basic salary was £64,766 in January 2010. A backbencher will be paid extra for chairing a committee, but not for being a member of one.
- Office support and living expenses, and travel to and from the constituency, are paid if the backbencher's constituency is outside London.
- The whole issue of MPs' and peers' expenses remains under review in the light of the expenses scandal of 2009.

2.5 The role of speaker of the House of Commons

The speaker of the House of Commons is always an MP of considerable seniority, elected by the other MPs. The speaker at the time of writing is John Bercow. He was elected in 2009 after his predecessor felt he had to resign over his

handling of the MPs' expenses affair. He has the responsibility of managing the House of Commons and acting as the MPs' spokesperson. He chairs all major debates (except for those on the Budget) and decides who may speak in which debates. He also has the role of keeping order in the House of Commons, and deciding whether to allow special emergency debates in the event of a crisis. The speaker has a vital role in ensuring that all MPs have the chance to speak, that the opposition gets the chance to criticise the government, and that minority parties can also play a role in Parliament. Although when first elected the speaker is a 'normal' MP, with a party background, he or she is expected to treat all parties equally and to behave in a totally impartial manner. The role becomes much more challenging in a 'balanced' or 'hung' Parliament, when issues such as membership of committees and priority in debates become much more difficult.

2.6 The role of party in the House of Commons

The importance of parties

As noted above, there is frequently a debate as to whether MPs are constituency representatives (agents who are free to vote as they see fit) or party delegates (committed to obeying party instructions). For most of the time, most MPs do as they are instructed by their parties, so party plays a huge role in Parliament. MPs of all parties receive weekly instructions from their whips (party managers in Parliament) telling them when and how to vote. The speaker will manage debates to ensure that there is fair representation from all parties. Committees of the House of Commons are always organised on party lines. It is loyalty to the party line that is most likely to ensure promotion to ministerial rank. Disloyalty to the party can lead to expulsion from the party (which is what happened to Ken Livingstone) and thus put an end to an MP's career in Parliament. Party is the single most important factor influencing the conduct of all MPs.

The need for parties

Without party organisation and loyalty it would be very difficult for the government of the day to get major measures through Parliament. There are about 100 members of the government in the House of Commons, who, if they disobey the whips, can expect to be sacked or have to resign, and thus lose their ministerial salary and chances of promotion. With 650 MPs in total, this does not give the government a majority, so it needs the support of the other governing party members in the House of Commons to get potentially unpopular measures through. The whips argue that an MP is elected because of her or his party 'label', and therefore the first loyalty of the MP should be to the party in Parliament. Some independent-minded MPs argue that they should have more freedom to vote according to their conscience or the needs of their constituents.

> Is it wrong to allow parties to have so much influence over Parliament?

Party discipline and conflicts of loyalty

A major reason for the defeat of the Conservatives in the 1997 election was the open divisions between the Conservative government of John Major and many of his backbench MPs. As a result, Tony Blair, Gordon Brown and their whips tried to maintain very tight discipline over Labour backbench MPs between 1997 and 2010 in order to keep an appearance of unity, seen as vital for winning elections. This was not always successful, as in the parliamentary session of 2004–05 when there were a total of 58 Labour backbench revolts, and the Prevention of Terrorism Bill of 2005 had Labour MPs voting against it a total of 27 times. The obvious divisions within the Parliamentary Labour Party after the election of Gordon Brown as party leader in 2007 also played a significant role in the 2010 election results. There were more backbench revolts under Gordon Brown between 2007 and 2010 than Tony Blair had between 1997 and 2007, which gave the impression of disunity and division.

Consider the difficult position of a backbench MP from the governing party who is a member of a select committee monitoring the performance of a government department. She feels that the minister (from the same party as her) and the department he is in charge of have acted incompetently. Should she highlight this and embarrass the party of which she is a member, and the government of which she would love to be a member? This highlights the problems arising from the lack of separation of powers in the UK system and the conflicting demands on MPs.

2.7 The role of party whips in the House of Commons

- Whips are members of the government and paid a salary in addition to their salaries as MPs. There is a chief whip, with several assistant whips.
- The opposition also has a whip system, and their chief whip is paid an additional salary in recognition of his or her contribution to the management of Parliament.
- Their principal role is to ensure the loyalty and attendance of backbenchers.
- They have a key role in the management of the business of the Commons, ensuring attendance at votes, debates and committees.
- They have also a vital role in communicating between government/shadow cabinet and backbenchers.
- Independent-minded MPs invariably complain that whips have too much power, but supporters of the whip system argue that little would happen in Parliament without the whips enforcing a degree of discipline.
- There is a whip system in the House of Lords, but the whips have less power.

2.8 The role of the opposition in the Commons

Once it was argued that the role of the opposition in Parliament was to 'oppose everything and propose nothing'. However, the role is:
- to provide alternative policies, legislation and government
- to use Question Time and adjournment debates to challenge and check the executive
- to hold the prime minister to account at Prime Minister's Question Time on Wednesdays
- to play a key role in all debates on legislation, both in the second reading and in the committee stage; the role of the shadow minister is very important here
- to turn up and vote

- to play a significant role in all parliamentary committees and chair committees; it is always a member of the opposition who chairs the key Public Accounts Committee
- to participate in the Westminster Hall debates

The opposition is given 20 parliamentary days for debating topics of their choice. They will usually choose issues which might embarrass the government. In 2008–09 they chose capital spending and Gurkha rights, for example.

Consider how important an effective opposition is to our democracy.

2.9 Law making in Parliament

A major part of the work of Parliament lies in making legislation. This legislation can be of vital national importance (e.g. a law to take the UK into the EU) or it can be a minor matter (e.g. a law dealing with the labelling of Scotch whisky) which affects relatively few people.

There are two main types of legislation:
- The vast majority of laws are government bills put forward by the government of the day.
- Other laws are put forward by ordinary backbench MPs — these are called private members' bills.

2.10 Government bills

A bill is a proposal for legislation to be put to Parliament. Ministers often request more bills than there is parliamentary time for, so a cabinet committee decides which bills will go before Parliament in the coming session and their order of priority. Clearly the prime minister will have a lot of influence over this.

Queen's Speech
The bills are listed in the Queen's Speech, which is written for the queen by No 10. It is then the job of the leaders of the House of Commons and Lords (both members of the cabinet) and the whips to get the bills through Parliament. Note the way in which this process is dominated by the government. This shows very clearly how the executive dominates Parliament.

First reading
This means the simple announcement to the House of Commons that a bill on a particular subject (e.g. the compulsory wearing of seatbelts) is coming. Printed copies of the bill are made available for everyone to scrutinise. This gives pressure groups and other opponents or supporters of the bill the opportunity to study it, to get organised and to brief MPs for or against it.

Second reading
This is the most important stage in the passage of a bill, usually taking place a few weeks after the formal first reading. The relevant minister (the transport minister in the case of seatbelts) will introduce the bill and argue for its support. The opposition spokesperson and backbenchers are then given ample opportunity to debate the measure, and at the end of the day a vote is taken. If it succeeds, this means that the House accepts the bill in principle. In the case of a normal bill, MPs will usually follow their party instructions on how to vote. When the government has a majority, a government bill invariably passes.

Evaluate Parliament
as a law maker. How
could the process
be improved?

There is limited scope for the opposition or backbenchers to achieve much in the way of preventing a bill or amending it if the government has a reliable majority who obey the whips.

Committee stage

The bill then goes to a standing committee — a group of backbench MPs whose role is to examine the bill in detail and make any necessary changes (e.g. allowing milk delivery people not to put on a seatbelt every time they get into their vehicles). It is usual for the principles behind the bill to remain unchanged. The majority of the committee always comprises members of the party of government, and the chair of the committee is also a member of the majority party in the Commons. On the whole, they do as the whips tell them. This is another example of the way in which the executive dominates Parliament. It is argued that Parliament cannot do its job of legislating properly with the whips so obviously 'on'.

MPs on the standing committee may not have any expertise in the relevant area; nor are they paid extra for such work. Although committee work is vital to improve bills, which may have been drawn up hurriedly, little status is given to such work by MPs and it is unlikely to improve their chances of promotion. Moreover, standing committees do not have the additional resources that their counterparts in the EU or the USA enjoy to carry out detailed research on bills and to question ministers and civil servants on them.

Report stage

If major changes are made by the standing committee, the House of Commons has to agree to them. A government with a majority invariably gets its way.

Third reading

This is usually just a formality and there is no debate.

Lords and royal assent

The bill must then be dealt with by the House of Lords and approved by the monarch before it becomes the law of the land. The House of Lords can be a major obstacle to the passage of a bill.

2.11 Private members' bills

Every year in Parliament a certain amount of time is set aside for legislation put forward by ordinary backbenchers. As so many wish to put forward a bill, those who are allowed to use the limited time available are chosen by ballot, and not on grounds of importance. Some very important laws, such as the abolition of capital punishment, the decriminalisation of homosexual acts and major changes in the divorce law have taken this route.

Governments prefer to avoid introducing legislation like this, as they can tend to lose the government party votes in subsequent elections. However, private members' bills can be very difficult to pass and are easy to block. For example, a bill to ban hunting with dogs was lost despite widespread support in the Commons and outside Parliament. Many feel that important issues such as those mentioned above should not be so dependent on the luck of a ballot and limited parliamentary time. In the parliamentary session 2003–04, five

of the 38 Acts of Parliament made were put forward by backbench MPs, and they covered issues such as Christmas Day opening of shops, the regulation of gangmasters, and protection of carers.

Criticisms

The main criticisms of private members' bills are as follows:

- They are chosen by ballot and not by importance.
- Major measures should not just be left to chance.
- Parliament should play a greater role in setting its own agenda.
- Although there are technically 'free' votes on such bills, the government and its whips are not averse to putting pressure on MPs to vote in a particular way.
- Such bills are easy to destroy on technicalities.
- They tend to be heard on a Friday, when many MPs have returned to their constituencies.

Rarely more than three pass in a year, but if it is a measure which the government wishes to support, and it does not have time itself, the bill stands a good chance of passing. In 2010 the MP Julie Morgan got through a private member's bill banning sunbeds for the under-18s, as there had been cancer-related concerns over their use. Government support was important here.

Of the 20 MPs who got ballot places in the 2007–08 session, three passed (numbers 1, 2 and 9 on the ballot). One was put forward by Michael Fallon MP — a Planning and Energy Bill which required new developments to be more environmentally friendly, which again had government support.

2.12 Standing committees

These are groups of backbench MPs who have the role of examining a bill in detail. Bills come to a standing committee after they have passed their second reading. Although no member of the government may be a member, there is always a government majority on the committee, and the chair is also a member of the majority party. If there is no majority, then membership reflects the balance of the House of Commons. It is very unusual for a standing committee to make any significant changes to the principles behind a bill, but it may make many amendments (changes). It may call the relevant ministers or civil servants to explain items, and it may occasionally call outside experts. The whips are 'on', so the government almost invariably gets its way. If the government is in a hurry, it is possible to cut short the discussion in committee by use of a procedural device called a guillotine, even when only a small amount of the bill has been examined. The bill is then returned to the Commons for the report stage and the third reading.

Do not confuse the different types of committee.

2.13 Select committees

Gladstone created the first select committee, the Public Accounts Committee, in the 1860s. Select committees are groups of backbenchers who have a responsibility for examining the work of a department, such as the Home Office, or for looking at a specific area, such as the ombudsman or the public accounts. The committee membership is usually 11 backbench MPs.

TOPIC 9 Parliament, the House of Commons and the House of Lords

As with standing committees, no member of the government may be a member, but most of the MPs on the committee will be from the majority party, if there is one. The majority party will also provide most of the chairs of the committees, and chairs dominate the committees' agenda. Membership, and the allocation of chairs, reflects the balance of the House of Commons. Chairs are paid an additional allowance, but ordinary members do not get one, so there is no financial incentive for their work.

The main purpose of the select committees is to provide a means of scrutinising the government and other public institutions, such as the television companies and the railways, and of upholding the public interest.

Merits of select committees

They have the right to request ministers and civil servants to appear before them, and the evidence that they give is, of course, televised and reported. Naturally, ministers and civil servants do not wish to appear incompetent in front of Parliament and the cameras, so they keep on their toes. Committees can also highlight deficiencies in government, and focus the attention of government on real problems. Examples of where select committees have encouraged government to act are:

- the safety of RoRo ferries
- caring for Gulf War veterans suffering from 'Gulf War Syndrome'
- providing sufficient customs officers at some ports to prevent drug smuggling
- ensuring a reduction in number of deaths in police custody on Saturday nights
- highlighting the Bank of England's failure to regulate banks

Demerits of select committees

The main failing of select committees is that the majority of MPs on them are members of the same party as the government of the day, and they are bound to have difficulty in criticising government measures openly. These committees also do not have the power to compel ministers or civil servants to attend, answer questions or provide information. They have no power over legislation — they can point out failings, but they cannot enforce solutions. They do not have the resources to call on experts. Really able MPs are not interested in working for them, as they do not lead to becoming a minister. No additional pay is given to an MP who chooses to sit on a select committee (except for the chair). There was strong criticism of the government in 2001 when it tried to prevent potential critics within its own party from sitting on select committees.

Should parliamentary committees be given more power?

A typical select committee's agenda

The Select Committee on Home Affairs in early 2010 reviewed government policy on, and made recommendations, on:

- the DNA database
- crime prevention
- the cocaine trade
- extradition to the USA
- police numbers

In order to develop its policy recommendations the committee interviewed:

- ministers
- civil servants and intelligence officers

- police chiefs
- lawyers
- journalists
- ministers of religion
- community leaders
- local government officials
- academic experts

The committee reports, and the government must respond to its report within 60 days. The committee's reports can also be discussed in the Westminster Hall debate, in which case the relevant minister has to attend and respond to the issues raised by the committee.

Much of the effectiveness of a select committee depends on the issue and on the ability of the chair and committee to get publicity and to pressurise the government and ministers.

The Public Accounts Committee

Perhaps the most influential of the select committees is the Public Accounts Committee, which is always chaired by a senior member of the opposition. This committee has the power to summon civil servants and make them answer for the spending of their department. It has the support of the National Audit Office, which employs a large number of skilled accountants and, with its reports and investigative capacity, ensures minimal dishonesty and incompetence in UK government.

2.14 The scrutiny role of the House of Commons

It is important to emphasise the main methods by which the Commons can scrutinise or check the actions of the government. These are:
- asking questions of ministers — written and oral
- debates and adjournment debates on specific issues
- opposition debates — part of 20 allocated for each session of Parliament, in which the opposition chooses the topic and the relevant ministers have to attend and respond
- emergency debates — decided by the speaker
- debates on legislation and Westminster Hall debates
- motions of no confidence in the government
- standing committees, checking the details of proposed legislation
- select committees, monitoring government departments and policy
- letters to ministers concerning constituents or constituencies
- referring matters to the ombudsman

Many of these areas have already been described, so we will concentrate here on the roles of parliamentary questions and debates, and of the parliamentary commissioner for administration.

2.15 Questions and debates

Each main parliamentary day starts with questions to ministers. The normal procedure is for two ministers to be questioned every day. MPs put down their questions in advance, but are allowed to ask a supplementary or additional question. Ministers are obliged to attend and deal with issues relating to

Be prepared for a question on the effectiveness of parliamentary scrutiny.

their department, and accept responsibility for it. The requirement to answer questions makes a minister keep fully up to date with the main work of the department, as the supplementary question is usually designed by opposition backbenchers to try to catch the minister out in public. It makes ministers really monitor what their department does. For example, on 14 January 2010 the secretary of state for business, innovation and skills was questioned on a variety of topics concerning his department, such as the future of the Royal Mail, new universities and the minimum wage.

There are also many opportunities for debates. Each bill is debated comprehensively in its second reading, and further debates take place when the opposition uses its time to debate an aspect of government policy (e.g. the government's foreign policy). Remember also that each day ends with an adjournment debate, when an MP can raise a matter that affects his or her constituency with a minister. (On 14 March 2010 the adjournment debate was used by an MP to raise with the minister for Europe the issue of a constituent who was in prison in Greece.) There can be emergency debates during times of crisis.

> Use the Parliamentary Channel on television to get examples of Parliament scrutinising the executive.

2.16 The ombudsman

Known formally as the parliamentary commissioner for administration, the ombudsman was intended to be the means by which ordinary citizens could obtain redress for their grievances against an incompetent executive (e.g. quickly retrieving an overpayment of tax). However, the civil service managed to reduce the powers that it was proposed to give the ombudsman, and grievances can only be referred to the ombudsman through an MP. Even then the ombudsman has very limited powers to investigate complaints, punish incompetence or even compensate citizens who have been unfairly treated. The office is often felt to be a waste of public money. Aspects of the work of the government recently investigated by the ombudsman have included child support payments, failure to repay tax, and the lack of dental care for the disabled. In these and other cases, a government department was required to make amends, and complied.

2.17 Parliament and the EU

The impact on Parliament of EU membership has been extensive. You need to be aware that:

- the sovereignty of Parliament has been reduced
- the ability to pass some legislation has gone to Brussels
- many regulatory powers have gone to Brussels
- ministerial responsibility to Parliament has changed, as decisions that UK ministers would have taken in the past have gone to Brussels
- the principle of accountability has changed
- there is a European Scrutiny Committee of the House of Commons which monitors all major new rules and regulations coming out of Brussels and the work of UK ministers in their respective councils

2.18 Parliament and devolution

Devolution to Scotland, Wales and Northern Ireland has also led to changes for the UK Parliament:

- Specific powers were devolved to Scotland, Wales and Northern Ireland after referendums in 1997 and 1998.
- Control in specific areas, such as education, was transferred to devolved government in Scotland, Wales and Northern Ireland.
- The Westminster Parliament is no longer responsible in specified areas, such as policing in Northern Ireland.

Devolution raises certain issues which need to be known:

- The 'West Lothian Question'. Should MPs for Scottish constituencies be able to vote on specifically 'English' issues in the UK Parliament?
- Should there be fewer Scottish/Welsh/Northern Irish MPs, as there is no 'English' Parliament?

2.19 Key issues

- MPs pay and expenses — this damaged the reputation of Parliament in general and the House of Commons in particular.
- Control over foreign policy — the wars in Iraq and Afghanistan. Should the executive be able to go to war without specific parliamentary permission?
- The whole question of parliamentary scrutiny and control over the executive.
- The role of the House of Commons when no single party has a majority.

2.20 Suggestions for the reform of the House of Commons

- Introducing election of MPs by proportional representation and giving constituents the power to throw out MPs during the life of the Parliament.
- Giving greater powers to both standing and select committees to alter legislation and monitor policy.
- Giving Parliament greater control over policy as opposed to just legislation.
- Ending the 'separation of powers', thus ending the **executive's domination** of Parliament.
- Reducing the powers and influence of the whips and giving greater autonomy to MPs, and enabling the Commons to set their own agenda.

Executive dominance: the situation which exists when the government (the executive) has considerable control over the legislature and the judiciary.

The House of Lords

3.1 Early developments

Originally the House of Lords was one of three Houses of Parliament. At the end of the fifteenth century it merged with the House of Clergy. From 1500 onwards it had equal status to the House of Commons, although it was smaller and its members were not elected. Membership was either by inheriting a title, such as an earldom, or being made a peer by the monarch. As early as the sixteenth century, however, it was the elected House of Commons that tended to take the initiative against the monarch in matters of policy, with the Lords being a much more conservative body that tended to support the monarch. This role lasted well into the nineteenth century.

3.2 Changes in the nineteenth and twentieth centuries

By the end of the nineteenth century, the House of Lords was playing a minor role in government. The convention was that it should play no part in money bills, and just agree to what the democratically elected House of Commons wished. When it came to non-money bills, the convention was that if the government of the day had a clear mandate for a bill (it had been in the governing party's manifesto and the party had then won an election), the House of Lords should allow the Commons bill to pass, after due deliberation. However, when the Lords rejected Home Rule for Ireland in the 1890s, for which the government had a clear mandate, and also rejected a Budget in 1909, they had to be reformed.

3.3 Reform of the House of Lords in the twentieth century

The first major reform of the Lords was the Parliament Act of 1911. This prevented the Lords exercising a veto (the power to reject) on any money bill, and only allowed the Lords to delay other bills for three sessions (years) of Parliament. There was no change to the membership of the Lords, which continued to consist of hereditary peers, bishops of the Church of England (not Catholics) and the Law Lords.

The delaying power was further reduced in the Parliament Act of 1949, to one session. Other changes included the Life Peerage Act of 1958, by which the prime minister was empowered to give people of either sex the right to sit and vote in the Lords in their own lifetime. The titles of these life peers did not pass down to the eldest son. An act of 1963 gave hereditary peers the right to give up their hereditary peerages.

3.4 The composition of the House of Lords

Until 1998 there were several different types of member of the House of Lords:
- There were about 634 hereditary (male) peers, who held their seats there because they had inherited a title. Many of these did not use their right to sit, vote and debate in the Lords.
- There were 479 life peers, appointed by the prime minister for life only, who included women. These also included the Law Lords — the top judges — who had taken over the old judicial functions of the House of Lords.
- There were 26 Church of England bishops and archbishops.

These were presided over by the Lord Chancellor, who was also a member of the cabinet.

In the Labour government's House of Lords Act 1999, the right of the hereditary peers to sit, debate and vote was abolished. A few hereditary peers remain until a further major reform of the Lords takes place. At present there are about 750 members of the Lords, comprising about 630 life peers, 26 Church of England bishops and archbishops (but no other faiths), and 92 elected hereditary peers.

Appointment now takes place in the following ways:
- Selection by the House of Lords appointments committee — an independent and non-partisan body which selects appropriate non-partisan people (the 'people's peers').

If the question is about 'Parliament', you need to mention the Lords as well as the House of Commons.

- Being made a peer by the monarch, on the recommendation of the prime minister. This is becoming very rare.
- Inclusion in the 'political list', used by party leaders to get working peers who will deal with legislation and committee work in the Lords.
- One-off creations by the prime minister in order to be able to appoint the people concerned as ministers — for example, Lords Mandelson, Sugar and Jones (by Gordon Brown), and Baroness Farsi, the first Muslim woman in the cabinet (by David Cameron).

Consider whether the UK actually needs a second chamber at all.

3.5 The present role of the House of Lords

Given that there is no written constitution that specifies the role of the Lords, custom plays a part. It ought to be stressed that different writers might advocate different views here. It is worth noting that the debate on the Lords and its reform has mainly centred on its membership and not on its functions. The main functions of this second chamber are as follows:

Scrutinising the work of the executive

The House of Lords has a Question Time, and every government department has one peer linked to it who will answer questions.

Debating bills

All bills have to be passed by both the Lords and the Commons.

Revising bills carefully

Sometimes the House of Commons may not have had time to deal with a bill properly. The Lords have been known to make dozens of major amendments to bills to improve them. Pressure groups often rely on the Lords to make changes to bills, especially when they cannot get access to Commons standing committees. Look, for example, at the committee stage in the Lords of the 2010 Equality Bill. There was no guillotine in operation, and there was very careful (and caring) study, line by line, of a bill and its implications.

Delaying bills

The Lords may feel that a particular proposal is wrong or unnecessary and may therefore act to delay its passage. This is an area where the Lords most often come into conflict with the government, as the Lords are accused of holding up the will of the elected part of the legislature. This ability to delay is one of the main reasons why governments are reluctant to give more power to the House of Lords. The lack of power in the Lords is probably a major reason why many people do not want to become members of it.

Checking a government

A government that had a majority in the Commons would be able to steamroller its programme through if the Lords had no power to stop it. Look carefully at the work of the House of Lords on the issues of:

- fox hunting
- the reform of the Lords and the role of the Lord Chancellor
- the Prevention of Terrorism legislation

Dealing with non-controversial matters

Many non-controversial issues require legislation, and the involvement of the Lords saves the Commons a lot of time.

Examining bills and debating policy in a non-partisan manner

Although many of the members of the Lords take a party whip, there are few ways in which they can be disciplined for disobeying it. Many others do not take a whip, and since all peers have no electors to worry about, they are in a position to speak and vote freely.

Debating major and controversial issues

The Lords can debate controversial subjects such as genetic engineering and the age of consent without concern for political parties or the electorate. The House of Commons is often worried about debating such issues, as MPs fear that what they say might offend their electors or their party bosses.

Debating and examining European legislation

The House of Commons does not seem to wish to undertake the detailed examination of EU legislation.

Providing ministers

The Lords is able to provide the government with ministers who do not have to worry about constituents (e.g. Baroness Amos, the first black woman in the UK cabinet, as secretary of state for international development in 2003). This is a good way of bringing possible talent into the government. Gordon Brown got Peter Mandelson back into the government in 2009 by making him a peer.

Fulfilling representative/expert roles

Prime ministers will often use their power to create peers in order to bring into public life members of groups which can be under-represented, such as women, ethnic minorities and gay people. They may also bring in experts in fields such as education, medicine and science.

3.6 Criticisms of the House of Lords

Several criticisms were levelled at the unreformed House of Lords, in terms of both the membership and the role.

- The main criticism was the method of selection. The fact that your grandfather had the cash to buy a peerage from Lloyd George in 1921, or your great-grandfather was a brilliant general, was no reason why you should be in the Lords. Also, being a man's eldest son was not a good criterion.
- The system seemed to be both sexist and racist, with few women or members of ethnic minorities in the Lords.
- There were Church of England bishops in the Lords, but no Catholic bishops or leaders of any other religious faith, so selection for the Lords discriminated on religious grounds as well.
- The Conservatives tended to dominate, and many of the hereditary peers only came to the Lords when requested to by the Conservative whips to vote for Conservative measures, or against Labour measures.

Consider whether is it undemocratic to have an unelected part of the legislature if it is actually representative.

- The Lords did not seem to do much. They seemed relatively powerless, and the bulk of their work was doing things that the House of Commons should really have been doing.
- Peers were not paid, but they received quite a generous attendance allowance and expenses if they turned up. They did not have to vote, speak or actually take part in any way in order to receive these payments. Several peers were strongly criticised, and one put on trial, over their expenses claims.

3.7 Reform of the House of Lords

Attempts were made to reform the Lords in both the 1960s (the Crossman reforms) and the 1970s (the Home reforms), but they broke down for several reasons:

- No one could agree, first, on whether reform was actually needed, and second, on whether it was just the membership of the Lords that needed to change or its role as well.
- There was no consensus on whether peers should be elected or appointed.
- The House of Commons was very reluctant to give up any power, and the executive was reluctant to make changes that might reduce its powers.
- It occurred to some that if you started to get rid of the hereditary principle behind much of the membership of the House of Lords, the idea might catch on with the monarchy as well.
- The changes would have to be written down in an act of Parliament, and logic might then dictate that a written constitution had to be produced which covered everything else.

Governments found it was simpler to do nothing.

3.8 The House of Lords Act, 1999

The Labour government elected in 1997 was committed to the reform of the House of Lords. It was a major item in the party's manifesto. On election, the prime minister set up a cabinet committee, chaired by the Lord Chancellor, Lord Irvine, to recommend reforms. There was some concern that the reform of the Lords had been handed over to its most important member (and speaker), and that 'outsiders' might bring a more democratic approach to bear.

The first result was the House of Lords Act 1999, which:

- removed the right of the hereditary peers to sit and vote in the Lords, with the exception of 92 'transition' hereditary peers who would be elected by the other departing hereditary peers; these transition peers would gradually be phased out entirely
- left 527 life peers, who would make up the main membership of the reformed House of Lords
- left the 26 bishops and archbishops of the Church of England and 27 Law Lords (who have since gone as a result of the Constitutional Reform Act 2005)

3.9 The Wakeham Commission

The Labour government then set up a royal commission to investigate the whole issue and recommend changes. A royal commission is a group of individuals, chosen by the government, who are given the role of investigating an issue and recommending policy changes. It is customary for a government to take very seriously the recommendations of a royal commission and make them law.

This royal commission was chaired by Lord Wakeham, a life peer who had been a senior minister under Margaret Thatcher in the 1980s. There was strong criticism from those who wished for a radical change, because both the chair and the members of the royal commission were very 'conservative' types, seen as unlikely to recommend anything too radical. The commission was asked to examine both the role and the membership of the House of Lords. When it published its report in 2000, it made the following recommendations:

- The changed House of Lords should bring experience and expertise, in areas such as agriculture, the armed services, social services and business, to the political process.
- It should be more representative, meaning that it should represent different social, ethnic and regional groups. This also implied that there should be an elected element.
- It should reflect the views of the regions of England and the nations of Scotland, Wales and Northern Ireland. Care should be taken to ensure that residents of those areas were in the Lords.
- It should help to check the executive — but the report was very vague about how this could or should be done.
- It should be largely appointive, its members chosen by the prime minister or by an independent group. This inevitably caused major debate, as it was hardly a democratic idea.
- There should be some elected members, but they should be a minority. The majority should be appointed.
- It should not be dominated by parties. It was hoped to develop a much more non-partisan atmosphere in the Lords, so that issues and bills could be looked at on their merits and not as a means of scoring points against another party.
- There should be no increase in the powers of the Lords. Inevitably this raised the issue of whether able men and women would wish to become members if they did not have the prospect of exercising much influence.
- Members should hold their seats for terms of 15 years, not for life.
- Religions in addition to the Church of England should be represented. In an increasingly secular age and an increasingly multi-faith society, this caused debate over which religions should be represented.
- The Lords should have a particular brief for civil liberties. This was a popular suggestion, but what it actually meant in practice was not explained. No additional powers were to be given which might help it to achieve a greater focus on civil liberties in the UK.

Several criticisms of the recommendations were made:

- The members of the royal commission were reluctant to change the powers of the House of Lords and wished to see the continuing dominance of the House of Commons and the executive in the whole political process.
- There would be a minority of elected members in the Lords.
- There was no mechanism for further scrutiny of the government.

- Given the scope of the changes, it was felt that there would be little change in the UK constitutional process.
- The appointments since made by the prime minister and the leader of the opposition have indicated that they wish to have the same type of person in the House of Lords as has been the case with life peers in the past.

3.10 Developments since the 1999 Act

The 1999 Act was seen very much as the first stage in reforming the House of Lords, but little actual progress has been made.

- The Queen's Speech of 2003 promised a bill to end the appointment of hereditary peers and to create an independent appointments commission to select non-party members for the Lords.
- In March 2004 the decision was taken to drop the bill, partly because of poor drafting, partly because of the amount of opposition it would cause, and partly because of the amount of both government and parliamentary time which it would consume on what was not felt to be an important issue.
- Serious divisions still exist within the government, the opposition, and Parliament generally over both the possible powers and the methods of selection and/or election to the second chamber.
- For the first time Conservatives do not dominate the House of Lords.

Various other possible reforms of the Lords have been suggested, some of which appeared on a small scale in party manifestos in 2010, especially that of the Liberal Democratic Party. None has really tackled the issue of what additional powers might be given to a 'better' or elected House of Lords. Suggestions for further reform have included:

- no second chamber at all (an option preferred by the very radical left)
- direct election for Lords, possibly on a regional basis using a type of proportional representation
- ending party domination of the Lords and deliberately not using party labels
- reforming the membership by:
  - making it elective
  - making it non-partisan
  - making it more representative regionally and in other ways, so that it 'looks like the UK'
  - ending the domination of the 'professional politicians' of the House of Commons

All these are rather vague and unlikely to happen. Reform of the Lords is the sort of issue that is divisive and time-consuming and can be put off while crises are dealt with.

In their manifestos for the 2010 general election both Labour and the Liberal Democrats argued for a fully elected House of Lords. The Conservatives did not mention the issue.

All three exams boards expect a degree of knowledge on this topic. Edexcel and AQA have it as a compulsory topic, while OCR has it as an optional topic. However, knowledge of the EU could well be important when dealing with other OCR topics, such as parties, the executive and the constitution, to name but three. Try also to rise above the strong anti-EU feelings generated by a large section of the UK press. It is not the terrible institution that it is sometimes made out to be.

> Try to avoid a very biased approach towards the EU.

To do well in this topic you need to:

- avoid the myth, rumour and media hostility to the EU: try to stay balanced
- grasp the way in which membership of the EU impacts on the legislatures, executives and judiciaries in the UK
- stay completely up to date with major EU developments and the UK's attitude towards them

Short questions

1 What is the role of the Council of Ministers and the European Council?
2 Describe the relationship between the European Parliament and the Westminster Parliament.
3 Why was the Lisbon Treaty seen as very important?
4 What is the role of the European Commission?

Essay questions

> Democratic deficit: the idea that so much power has gone to the unelected and unaccountable EU that the rights and liberties of UK citizens have suffered, as has the democratic process.

5 Assess the impact of membership of the EU on the UK constitution.
6 To what extent has membership of the EU led to a **democratic deficit** in the UK?
7 Discuss the UK's role in the decision-making process of the EU.
8 Discuss the view that membership of the EU has had an enormous impact on party politics in the UK.

1 The nature of the EU

- The present EU grew out of the EEC (the European Economic Community). This was set up by the Treaty of Rome, which came into effect in 1958.
- The first members were France, Germany, Italy, Belgium, Holland and Luxembourg.
- All six had suffered defeat in the Second World War by either the Nazis or the Allies and had been devastated by war.
- All six were united in their desire for peace, reconstruction, liberal democracy and the prevention of communism.
- All agreed that economic and political cooperation were the keys to achieving the four objectives above. This was the real purpose behind the EU's creation.

1.1 The aims and objectives of the EU

These have remained largely unchanged since the Treaty of Rome was signed. It is how they are attained that has changed. They are:

Always show awareness of the broader aims and objectives of the EU.

- peace for Europe
- prosperity for Europeans
- liberty for Europeans

2 *The history of the EU*

- 1958: the EEC is formed.
- 1962: a common agricultural policy is agreed in order to sustain farming, food prices and food production.
- 1963: the first EEC international agreement with former colonies shows the EEC working together in foreign affairs.
- 1968: free trade within the EEC is agreed. No more barriers to trade within the EEC.
- 1973: the six become nine as the UK, Ireland and Denmark join.
- 1974: the European Regional Development Fund is set up to aid poorer regions (Wales and Scotland are both major beneficiaries).
- 1979: first direct elections to the EU Parliament.
- 1981–86: Greece, Spain and Portugal join after becoming liberal democracies.
- 1986: the Single European Act is passed. Signed by Conservative prime minister Margaret Thatcher, it leads to the UK becoming much more integrated into the EU.
- 1993: the Single Market is created for all members of the EU.
- 1995: Austria, Finland and Sweden join.
- 1995: the Schengen Agreement is signed. It permitted free movement without passports for EU citizens throughout the EU.
- 2002: the euro is introduced; the UK stays out of the euro zone.
- 2003: the first EU peacekeeping force is deployed in former Yugoslavia.
- 2004–07: Poland and other Eastern European countries join; the EU grows to 27 members.
- 2007: the Lisbon Treaty is signed, resulting in further integration and more powers for the EU Commission and Parliament.

2.1 The UK's entry into the EU

- 1955–57: the UK refuses to join in setting up the EEC, in spite of receiving a strong invitation.
- 1958: the UK government realises that refusing to join was a serious error, and that membership would reverse economic decline.
- 1963: the first failed attempt to join, by the Conservatives under Macmillan.
- 1967: the second failed attempt to join, by Labour under Wilson.
- 1970: applying for membership of the EEC is in the Conservative manifesto, so when the Conservatives win the election they have a mandate for joining.
- 1973: the UK joins the EEC, taken in by the Conservatives under Heath.
- 1975: the first major referendum is held in the UK, and it confirms the UK's membership of the EEC.

Note that both the major parties were keen on joining the EU, but both were divided on the issue.

2.2 Key recent EU developments

- 1986: the Single European Act, which promised a free internal market by 1992 and brought in QMV (Qualified Majority Voting), ending national vetoes.
- 1990: the UK joins the ERM (exchange rate mechanism) — intended as a prelude to full monetary union in Europe.
- 1991: the Maastricht Treaty is signed by Conservative prime minister John Major:
  - The UK opts out of the Social Chapter, which extended the EU's role into employment rights/social protection.
  - The EU moves towards common foreign and security policy and common home affairs policy.
  - All citizens of the EU gain common European citizenship.
  - A pathway to economic and monetary union is set out.
  - More power is given to the European Parliament.
  - The **subsidiarity** principle is established, pushing decision making down to the lowest possible level.
  - There is further extension of QMV, weakening national vetoes.
  - The EU becomes much more a supranational organisation.
- 1992: the UK leaves the ERM after 'Black Wednesday', when an economic crisis hits the UK.
- 1997: the **Amsterdam Treaty** is signed by Labour prime minister Tony Blair:
  - The UK accepts the Social Chapter, giving more employment and social rights to citizens.
  - QMV is extended, again weakening the national vetoes and extending the power of the Council and Commission.
  - Further powers are given to the EU Parliament, including a veto in some areas.
- 2001: the **Nice Treaty** is signed:
  - QMV is extended further.
  - The number of MEPs is changed.
  - Changes are made to the power of the Commission, for example giving it greater powers of initiative.
  - The EU is generally strengthened as an organisation.
- 2004: the **Draft Treaty for Establishing a Constitution for Europe** is signed in Rome. The intention is to update the rules and regulations for running the EU and to bring about greater transparency.
- 2005: France and Holland reject the proposed European constitution by referendums.
- 2007: the **Lisbon Treaty** is signed by Labour prime minister Gordon Brown. It:
  - aims to make the EU more transparent, democratic and efficient
  - gives more powers both to the EU Parliament and to national parliaments over EU legislation
  - clarifies the relationship between national governments and the EU
  - extends QMV into further areas
  - reforms and makes more efficient the EU structure in the light of **enlargement**
  - creates a President of the EU Council, who is to be the leader of the EU

Subsidiarity: the system whereby decisions are made at the lowest possible level. The idea has been strongly emphasised from Maastricht onwards to deflect criticism of the EU in Brussels for being all-powerful. The idea is that decisions affecting localities are made within those localities by local people wherever possible.

Enlargement: the process of adding more members to the EU.

Note the gradual growth of both the power and influence of the EU.

    – starts a system of common foreign and security policy, with Lady Ashton of the UK appointed to the new post of high representative for foreign and security policy

3 *The institutions of the EU*

3.1 The European Council

- Contains all the elected heads of government of member states.
- Provides leadership for strategic issues, such as enlargement or a new constitution.
- Is the key decision taker for the future direction of the EU — but the meetings can be cantankerous media events which decide little.

3.2 The Council of Ministers

- This is the key decision maker in specific areas such as international trade or agriculture.
- All home secretaries/ministers of interior/justice ministers meet to decide on issues such as asylum or combating terrorism, and all ministers of agriculture and fisheries deal with fish stocks or food production.
- These ministers remain accountable, of course, to their own parliaments and electorates.
- The members of the Council are expected to protect the interests of their own nations as well as look at wider European needs.

3.3 The European Commission

- The 'civil service' of the EU.
- Has 27 Commissioners — one per member state (for example, the UK's Baroness is Ashton is vice-president of the Commission and responsible for foreign and security policy.
- Initiates legislation/policy for the EU.
- Carries out EU policy.
- Is expected to be 'European' and to rise above national interests.

Ensure you have a good working knowledge of the decision-making process within the EU.

3.4 The European Parliament

- Consists of 736 MEPs and is directly elected by the Europe-wide electorate every 5 years.
- The UK sends 72 MEPs to it.
- Groupings of MEPs are political, not national — e.g. left or right.
- The Parliament has a legislative role with the Council.
- It has the usual democratic controls over the rest of the EU system. For example, it can dismiss the Commission.
- It has budgetary control, except over the Common Agricultural Policy (CAP).

3.5 The European Court of Justice

- Is not to be confused with the European Court of Human Rights.
- Has 27 judges (two from the UK at present).

- Plays a key referee role in the EU between member states or between the EU and a member state.
- Interprets EU legislation and rules — which can make it into a law maker.
- Has primacy over UK law/judiciary (note the Factortame case, and free prescriptions for men as well as women over 60).

3.6 The decision-making process in the EU

- An idea emerges — within the scope of the EU's authority — such as tighter controls on car exhaust emissions.
- The relevant commissioner and department consult all stakeholders widely at first.
- The relevant council takes the decision to proceed with the idea.
- The Permanent Representative Committee (COREPER) discusses and consults member states.
- The European Parliament, pressure groups, national governments and parliaments, the Committee of the Regions, and the Economic and Social Committee are all consulted. The European Parliament has to agree.
- The final decision lies with the Council.

Be fully aware of what part UK citizens can and do play in the decision-making process of the EU.

4 The impact of EU membership on the UK

4.1 On Parliament

- Legislative **sovereignty** has gone, as EU laws can override UK-made laws.
- EU law is superior to that passed by Parliament.
- The UK Parliament did vote for accession to the EU and its growth, e.g. the Single European Act.
- It has a monitoring role over EU legislation, both before and after passage, but it is little used. The Commons leaves most of the work of checking EU legislation to the Lords.
- It can of course vote to leave the EU.

Overall there has been a substantial impact on the UK Parliament.

Sovereignty: the ultimate and final political authority, which cannot be overruled by anyone or any other body. It was always argued that sovereignty in the UK lay with Parliament. Once Parliament made a law everyone had to obey it, even the sovereign. As a result of membership of the EU, some of the UK 'sovereignty' has been transferred to the EU in certain specified areas. Parliament cannot overrule properly made EU legislation. This is a very likely area for questions, so make sure you get the details right.

4.2 On the executive

- Ministers and the civil service are directly involved in the EU Council and COREPER.
- Areas such as agriculture and international trade are now decided in Brussels, not by ministers and civil servants in London.
- There is a large EU dimension in areas such as environment and employment, so London (and the devolved assemblies and executives in Wales, Scotland and Northern Ireland) have to work with Brussels.
- Health, education, and law and order are largely left to national governments and local authorities to decide.
- The impact of QMV again reduces the power of national governments.

Overall there has been a very considerable impact on the UK executive.

4.3 On the constitution

National sovereignty: the concept that ultimate power lies within the nation. Critics of the EU argue that because so many major issues are now decided in Brussels the UK has lost its national sovereignty.

- The growing power of the executive and Brussels means parliamentary sovereignty has gone (although already a fiction).
- **National sovereignty** has gone (also a fiction?).
- The impact of subsidiarity is considerable, possibly preventing UK governments from taking centralisation action.
- Possibly it has made the UK more democratic, with, for example, membership of the European Parliament and the Human Rights Act.
- There is less accountability — can the minister responsible for agriculture be made to take responsibility for policy made by others in Brussels which he or she may have opposed?
- There is the impact of QMV on the decision-making process.
- There is the impact of the European Court of Justice and the European Court of Human Rights on key areas of the constitution.
- The regionalism stressed by the EU runs counter to the centralisation policy of recent UK governments.
- A European foreign and defence policy is being developed which may run counter to UK traditions and wishes.

How fundamentally has EU membership changed the UK constitution?

Overall there has been a substantial impact on the UK constitution.

4.4 On the judiciary and the law

- The rulings of the European Court of Justice have to be followed in the UK.
- The European Court of Human Rights (although technically not a part of the EU) and its rulings effect the rights and liberties of UK citizens greatly.
- It has led to the growing Europeanisation of the UK judiciary, for example with new ideas of proportionality.

Again there has been a substantial impact on the UK's judicial process.

4.5 On pressure groups

- The EU expects to be contacted by pressure groups and to work with them on legislation.
- Pressure groups have a formal role prior to decision taking within the EU.
- Major UK pressure groups have moved to Brussels, e.g. the NFU, trade unions, the CBI and environmental groups, as that is where key decisions are made.
- The EU has a small number of known key decision takers, so it is easy for pressure groups to contact and focus on these.

Pressure groups are well aware that many decisions are now made in Brussels, and that is where they focus their efforts, often making alliances with pressure groups in other European countries.

5 The impact of EU membership on UK parties

5.1 The Conservative Party

- It was a Conservative government that made the first unsuccessful attempt to join the EU.
- It was Heath, a Conservative prime minister, who took the UK into the EU in 1972, but he depended on Labour abstentions for the final successful vote.
- The party split over the referendum in 1975, with many Conservatives wishing to leave the EEC.
- Margaret Thatcher was always critical and suspicious of the EU, but put through the critical Single European Act.
- The EU was a highly divisive issue in the party in the last years of Thatcher's leadership, caused resignations and was a key cause of her fall in 1990. Many leading Conservatives became very hostile to the EU, while other figures such as Clarke, Lawson and Hurd were very strong supporters of the EU.
- Divisions over the EU and Maastricht Treaty dominated the Major premiership of 1990–97.
- Divisions over the EU in the cabinet and the parliamentary party played a significant role in the Conservative defeat in the 1997 election.
- Hague pushed opposition to the EU and the euro hard in the 2001 general election, but the public seemed uninterested in the topic.
- The party is still divided over the issue, but Cameron has downplayed it in order to ensure unity.
- The party has worried about losing votes to UKIP and the BNP over the EU.

Conservative policy in the 2010 election campaign

The Conservative Party's position on the EU in the 2010 general election campaign was that it:

- would definitely stay in, but would oppose any further move towards 'federalism'
- would be an 'active and energetic member' of the EU
- would not sign any more treaties like Lisbon without a referendum first
- would pass a UK Sovereignty Bill which stated clearly that UK sovereignty lies in the UK
- would end EU dominance in certain social/economic areas such as the Working Time Directive
- would stop EU judges extending their control over the UK criminal justice system
- would never join the euro

The Conservative Party was clearly aware of the underlying hostility to the EU and the influx of 'foreign workers', but was also well aware of the economic importance of EU membership. It made little mention of the EU in its campaign, apart from attacking the Liberal Democrats' policies.

Federalism: a system of government whereby there are usually two levels of government, each having sovereignty over specified areas. For example, in the USA the federal government in Washington, DC takes decisions in areas such as foreign policy, while the individual states take decisions (having sovereignty) in areas such as education.

Note very carefully the impact of the coalition government on the Conservative Party. The Liberal Democrats were always very enthusiastic supporters of the EU.

5.2 The Labour Party

- The party was badly divided over the EU between right and left initially, the left seeing the EU as a 'capitalist' or 'rich man's' club.
- Some opposed entry in 1972 and some voted for it, while others abstained.
- The party was so badly divided that collective responsibility was suspended over the issue, and Wilson called a referendum to decide it.
- Divisions within the party continued after the 1975 referendum, which was in favour of staying in the EEC.
- One reason for the Social Democratic Party (SDP) splitting from the Labour Party in 1981 was the desire of Foot and Benn to leave the EU.
- Kinnock developed a more positive attitude to the EU, helped by the rise of moderate socialism among EU leaders, so the left did not see the EU as hostile and felt it might improve the rights and conditions of workers in the UK.

Tony Blair:
- was always very positive towards the EU and played a constructive role within it, especially over the Amsterdam Treaty
- made the UK government much more positive towards the EU and insisted on real cooperation by the UK executive with the EU
- supported enlargement and the concept of an EU constitution
- was in favour of the economic development of the UK through membership of the EU; he was in favour of the euro, but was forced to back down by Brown and public opinion/media pressure
- failed to convince the UK public that the EU was a good idea and avoided a promised referendum on the Lisbon Treaty, as he knew he would probably lose given the hostility of the foreign-owned media towards it
- upset fellow EU members over his decision to invade Iraq
- failed to reform the EU budget

Gordon Brown:
- signed the Lisbon Treaty, eventually
- played a key role in the UK's decision not to join the euro
- always remained more suspicious of the EU than Tony Blair had been

Labour policy on the EU in the 2010 campaign

The Labour Party's manifesto for the 2010 general election made limited mention of the EU. It took a low-key approach to the issue, but was generally positive and supportive. Its main message was 'a strong Britain in a reformed Europe'. The party's position was that it:
- would retain EU social policies such as the Working Time Directive
- would reform the EU budget and the CAP
- would not join the euro without a referendum

5.3 The Liberal Democratic Party

- The party has always had a highly positive attitude towards the EU.
- It has had the most coherent policy towards the EU.
- It is in favour of a federal approach.
- It is a strong supporter of giving greater powers to the EU.

Note the differing policies of the major parties on the EU in the 2010 election: it was not a major issue.

Liberal Democratic policy on the EU in the 2010 campaign
The Liberal Democratic Party manifesto for the 2010 general election reflected a positive and enthusiastic commitment to the EU, but for electoral reasons the party did not stress it shortly.

5.4 The United Kingdom Independence Party (UKIP)

- The party is committed to withdrawal from the EU.
- The main reasons for its opposition are the cost of membership, the immigration which it believes results from membership, and the loss of sovereignty.
- In the election for MEPs in 2009 the party won 13 seats in the European Parliament.
- In the general election of 2010 the party fielded 630 candidates, advocating total opposition to the EU and advocating withdrawal from it.

5.5 The Scottish Nationalist Party (SNP) and Plaid Cymru (PC)

- Both parties were initially hostile to the EU, seeing it as a threat to nationalist aspirations.
- Now they are much more positive, because of the idea of greater power being given to bodies such as the Scottish and Welsh assemblies in the EU and the benefits they have gained through EU funds.
- They tend to avoid the issue as it can still be divisive.

5.6 The British National Party (BNP)

- The party strongly opposes the EU and would take the UK out of it.
- Its main reasons for this are similar to UKIP's, namely the loss of sovereignty and mass immigration.

6 Recent EU developments which need to be known

- The Lisbon Treaty and its impact on parties in the UK.
- The referendums in the EU on the EU constitution and their impact on Blair and Brown.
- The enlargement of the EU, particularly the debate on Turkish entry.
- The 2009 European election results.
- The role of the EU in the 2010 general election.
- The impact of the economic crisis in Greece on the EU, and UK attitudes towards the euro.

The judiciary, rights, liberties and the redress of grievances

Civil liberties: these are the freedoms that are, or should be, guaranteed to individuals in a state to protect them against harsh treatment. The right to silence and the right to a fair trial are typical 'civil liberties'.

Edexcel has the judiciary and **civil liberties** as a compulsory topic, with the focus on the role of the judiciary, the power and influence of judges, and rights and liberties. AQA also has the judiciary as a compulsory topic, but with the focus on judicial appointments, the role of the judiciary, and the relationship between the judiciary and the executive and the legislature. There could also be questions on the impact of the Human Rights Act and the European Convention on Human Rights on UK politics. OCR has the judiciary as an optional topic, with likely questions on the role of the judiciary, rights and liberties, and also the redress of grievances.

To do well on this topic you need to:

- make sure you get your terms right — that you can explain what 'judicial review' means and don't confuse it with 'judicial independence', for example
- ensure that you have not used an out-of-date textbook, as there have been big changes to the judiciary since the passing of the Constitutional Reform Act of 2005
- have a good list of recent cases/examples which you have looked up yourself — nothing is worse than every candidate in a centre dishing out the same out-of-date and often irrelevant example

Short questions

1 Explain how judges are appointed and dismissed.
2 Describe the principal changes brought about by the Constitutional Reform Act of 2005.
3 Explain what is meant by judicial review and judicial independence.
4 Explain what is meant by the separation of powers.

Essay questions

5 Discuss the view that judges have too much political influence.
6 To what extent are rights and liberties well defended in the UK?
7 Discuss the view that in spite of the Constitutional Reform Act of 2005, the judiciary still needs major reform.
8 To what extent have the Human Rights Act and the European Convention on Human Rights had a major impact on rights and liberties in the UK?
9 Discuss the view that getting grievances redressed in the UK is 'difficult, time consuming and very expensive'.

You will need to get your head round quite a lot of different concepts.

1 The role of the judiciary

Judges have six broad roles. With no written constitution, those roles can of course change over time, and often what judges get publicity for is not what they spend most of their time doing. Their main roles are as follows:

Law: a series of rules passed by any sovereign state.

- To interpret the **law**. The law may say that a person may use 'reasonable' force to defend themselves or their property. A judge has ruled that beating a burglar with a cricket bat and causing him brain damage was 'unreasonable', and imprisoned the man who attacked the burglar.

Judicial review: the power of a judge to examine the actions of the executive or anyone in a position of authority and rule whether or not those actions were lawful. It can now apply to laws passed by the Westminster and Scottish Parliaments.

- To administer the law and carry out the will of Parliament, managing trials in accordance with the law and sentencing in criminal cases. They act as the decision maker in most civil cases, such as a dispute between companies over a contract, or between parents over custody of children. Their role is basically to carry out the will of Parliament in legal matters in the same way as the executive carries out the will of Parliament in, for example, collecting the taxes voted for by Parliament.
- To carry out **judicial review**. This is the area which tends to attract most publicity. It means the judges 'review' or examine the actions of the executive (or others) and decide whether they acted within the law.
- To chair public inquiries. Often they are asked to chair major public inquiries into controversial issues and to report and make recommendations. For example, Dame Janet Smith looked at the Shipman mass murder case in 2005, and Lord Saville chaired the Bloody Sunday Inquiry, which dealt with the shooting of civilians by the army in Northern Ireland in 1972.
- To enforce EU law and the European Convention on Human Rights. In addition to enforcing UK laws, they have to ensure that the rules and regulations of the EU are implemented, and deal with occasions when EU law might conflict with UK laws. They also have to implement the European Convention on Human Rights, which now has the force of law in the UK as a result of the Human Rights Act of 1998.

Note the links between the role of the judiciary and UK politics.

- To debate, either in the Lords or elsewhere. Traditionally judges were not expected to speak outside their courts, but increasingly they have got involved in debates on relevant issues, such as those on assisted suicide or the age of consent, either in the Lords or in the media.

1.1 The importance of the judiciary/the power and influence of judges

If you are asked to write about why the judiciary is important in a democracy, or give an idea why judges are such important figures, here are some of the points you could make:

Judicial independence: an independent judiciary is one where the judges are free from control or pressure from the executive and legislature and can make their decisions without fear and on the basis of what they believe is appropriate in the circumstances of the case.

- They are **independent** of the executive and legislature and have a key referee role in our society.
- They uphold the vital principles of the rule of law, and ensure that all are equal under the law.
- They are very important upholders of our rights and liberties, and they have the job of interpreting the Human Rights Act and the European Convention on Human Rights.
- One branch of the judiciary has to make decisions about whom to prosecute and for what. In cases such as those concerning 'cash for honours' or MPs' and peers' expenses, this can have a huge political impact.

Looking at the vital roles the judiciary plays, you can see how important its independence is.

- Their decisions can have tremendous political impact, as has been seen in cases regarding asylum, immigration and detention without trial.
- They can be a serious brake on the executive, at all levels.
- They are often left to take decisions on issues that politicians prefer to ignore, such as assisted suicide.

1.2 The structure of the judiciary

Detailed knowledge of the structure of the whole judiciary is not required by any of the boards. At the top of the tree is the new (2009) Supreme Court. This court:

- is the final court of appeal for all UK civil cases, and criminal cases from England, Wales and Northern Ireland
- hears appeals on arguable points of law of general public importance
- concentrates on cases of the greatest public and constitutional importance
- maintains and develops the role of the highest court in the UK as a leader in the common law world

Under the Supreme Court are two Courts of Appeal, one for criminal cases, and the other for civil cases, which have been passed up from the Crown Courts (criminal) and the County and High Courts (civil). At the very bottom is the magistrate, who deals with about 98% of all criminal cases.

1.3 Judicial appointments and dismissals

Before the 2005 Constitutional Reform Act all judges were appointed and promoted by the Lord Chancellor (who would almost certainly involve the prime minister in the decisions on the top jobs). The Lord Chancellor was of course a member of the House of Lords (the legislature) and also a major figure in the government (the executive), thus representing a clear breach of the separation of powers principle. The appointment and promotion process was both secret and unaccountable. There were concerns that the judges appointed tended to be:

- male
- white
- from privileged backgrounds (public school and Oxbridge)
- out of touch with public opinion and attitudes
- too linked in to the political process
- unaccountable

The intention of the Constitutional Reform Act was to change this and broaden the intake. Now, lawyers who wish to become judges apply in response to advertisements. An independent and transparent Judicial Appointments Commission tests, vets and interviews them, and the Commission then makes a recommendation to the Crown for the advertised vacancy. The aim is also to reduce the power of the prime minister/executive to influence the judiciary.

Judges are still dismissed in the old way, by an address by both Houses of Parliament to the Crown. This has not happened.

1.4 The Constitutional Reform Act of 2005

This act is an excellent example for AS students. First, it demonstrates the power of the prime minister. Tony Blair pushed it in 2003 without there being much demand for it, and with limited consultation. Second, it changes the constitution fundamentally and is a very good example of how that happens. The key terms are as follows:

> Make sure you have a thorough working knowledge of the 2005 Act.

- Its aims include upholding the rule of law, ensuring judicial independence and reinforcing the separation of powers. It is not often that such constitutional principles are stated so firmly in an Act of Parliament.
- It changes the role of the Lord Chancellor from its previous judicial, as well as executive and legislative responsibilities, to one that is only executive and legislative, like that of any other minister. The office has also been reduced in status, with the post held in conjunction with that of secretary of state for justice by an MP, not a member of the Lords (Jack Straw in the Labour government in 2010, followed by Kenneth Clarke in the Conservative–Liberal Democratic coalition government).
- The Lord Chief Justice, a lawyer and not a politician, is now head of the judiciary.
- It created the new Supreme Court as the final court of appeal. This role is no longer fulfilled by the House of Lords (part of the legislature).
- Ministers are expressly barred from interfering in the judicial process.
- It makes enforcing the Human Rights Act and the European Convention on Human rights easier.

1.5 The separation of powers

Some great eighteenth-century thinkers argued strongly that one way to safeguard liberty and democracy was to ensure that the three 'powers' or parts of a system of government — the executive, the legislature and the judiciary — always remained completely separate. (The concept known as the separation of powers.) Nobody could be a member of more than one of these parts, and each part would play a role in checking the other. This way no one part, such as the executive, could get too much power and threaten liberty and democracy. The legislature could check the executive (always the biggest potential threat to freedom); the judiciary could ensure that the executive and legislators remained within the law, etc.

In theory this 'separation of powers' is part of our constitutional process, but of course it does not work in practice. By convention, members of the executive, the prime minister and cabinet, also have to be members of Parliament. They, of course, dominate Parliament and its agenda through the whips. Until recently the Lord Chancellor was not only in the cabinet (the executive), but was also speaker of the House of Lords (the legislature) and head of the judiciary. Note how the Constitutional Reform Act has changed this. Moves to make Parliament more free of the executive are under way, but the government's domination of Parliament means the relationship is still not what it should be in an ideal democracy.

1.6 Judicial neutrality

It is a convention that judges remain '**neutral**' as far as politics and political issues are concerned. This means they should not get involved in party politics at any level, and they should not be seen or heard to be commenting in any way which might be interpreted as favouring one party or its policies over another. That is fine in theory, but very difficult to work in practice.

Make sure you can define and explain these key concepts.

Judicial neutrality: the requirement that a judge be totally neutral and not take sides or sympathise with one side, in a case which might, for example, involve a member of the government. The judge is expected to ignore pressure from, for example, the media or ministers and judge the case solely on its merits.

- By the nature of their work in courts they may have to make decisions on issues such as police powers, asylum seekers and the length of sentences (as in the case of James Bulger's killers). These are all highly 'political' issues.
- They head public inquiries on highly 'political' cases such as the Bloody Sunday killings and the murder of Stephen Lawrence.
- It is very hard to separate '**justice**' from politics.
- It has become easier with the Constitutional Reform Act, since the head of the judiciary, who deals with the appointment and promotion of judges, is no longer a politician sitting in the cabinet.
- Increasingly judges are commenting on issues in both the House of Lords and the media.

However, check the roles of the secretary of state for justice and the Attorney General. They are both members of the executive and legislature and have 'legal' roles as well. Note the Attorney General's roles in declaring the Iraq war 'legal' as well as in challenging sentences made by judges.

> Justice: a principle of fairness or proper balance. There is a real difference between what is law and what is just. Justice is done to a criminal when there has been a proper trial, with a proper defence as well as prosecution, in front of an impartial judge with a properly chosen jury.

1.7 Judicial independence

It is vital in a democracy, where the rule of law is a central principle, that judges remain free of pressure from politicians. There will be times when judges and prosecutors make decisions (such as which MPs or peers to prosecute over expenses) that are going to upset politicians. Steps are taken to protect judges and prosecutors from external pressures, so that they can make decisions in accordance with the law without fear of being sacked or not paid or of missing out on promotion if they make the 'wrong' decision:

- They are paid from the Consolidated Fund, which means that politicians and civil servants cannot stop or adjust their pay.
- They are well paid, so they should not need to accept bribes.
- The new (2005) appointment and promotion process is independent and transparent.
- They have security of tenure: it is very difficult to fire them. This can only be done by an address of both Houses of Parliament — and that has not happened for centuries.
- Judges are expected to stay right out of politics and direct political involvement. In return, members of both Houses of Parliament and members of the executive do not comment on legal matters while trials are proceeding, and do not criticise sentences and rulings. In other words, judges stay out of politics and politicians stay out of the law.

However, the secretary of state for justice/Lord Chancellor and the Attorney General (politicians appointed by the prime minister) still have a role to play in the law, so the issue of how independent the UK judiciary is will remain.

1.8 Judicial review

Simply this means that a judge has the power to review or examine an action (usually of a member of the executive) and decide whether it is legal or not, or whether the person who took it has exceeded their powers. It does not have to be a 'political' action — in one case parents challenged the right (by asking for a judicial review) of a head teacher to stop a pupil returning to do their A-levels in a school.

(The parents lost!) The majority of applications for judicial review are rejected, and only a minority actually affect central government (most concern local government actions, such as planning decisions). However, some cases attract great publicity and can cause governments considerable irritation, hence the importance given to this topic in Politics exams. Issues which have been well publicised are:

- immigration and asylum seekers
- homelessness
- a ruling that the BBC did not have to have the leader of the SNP participating in the final leadership debate in the 2010 general election
- Belmarsh detainees
- the killers of Jamie Bulger
- attempts to prevent Gary McKinnon, a computer hacker, being extradited to the USA
- Greenpeace taking the government to court over the third runway at Heathrow.

There are concerns about the power given to unelected judges over elected and accountable politicians, as well as the cost of taking such cases to court.

1.9 The relationship between the judiciary, European courts and EU law

Membership of the EU has had a major impact on the UK's judiciary, as well as the executive and legislature. When we joined, the UK agreed to obey the rules of the club, just in the same way as a new football club agrees to adhere to the usual rules of football. This has the following consequences:

- Rulings by the European Court of Justice have the force of law in the UK, and judges have to enforce them.
- EU directives and EU legislation have the force of law in the UK, and again judges have to enforce them.
- There can be conflict between an Act of Parliament and an EU 'rule', with some lawyers arguing that through the sovereignty of Parliament judges should give the Act of Parliament priority over the EU rules.
- It does possibly give judges the power to strike down an Act of Parliament.

Note the two important examples of the Factortame case, which gave Spanish fishermen the right to fish in 'UK' waters, and the *ex parte* EOC (Equal Opportunities Commission) case, which was more important legally and gave many rights to part-time workers in the UK. Both involved a clash between UK and EU law, and EU law 'won'.

Rights and liberties

2.1 The development of rights and liberties in the UK

The custom in the UK was that individuals had the **right** to do what they wished unless there was a law against it. Sometimes Acts of Parliament were passed to take away rights, such as the freedom from arrest without due cause, in time of war. At other times, Parliament might pass a law giving citizens new rights, such as the 1872 law that gave the right to vote in secret. The rights and liberties of UK citizens never developed in an organised or systematic way. People were

---

Get your own recent examples of judicial review at work.

Make sure you are well aware of the difference between the EU Court of Justice and the European Court of Human Rights.

Rights: a right is the ability to do something which may be guaranteed by law. The European Convention on Human Rights gives everyone the right to marry. Some argue that some rights, such as the right to marry, are so fundamental that they cannot be taken away or altered in any way by laws passed by Parliament.

used to not having a clear definition of their rights, such as the Americans have in the first ten amendments to their constitution, known as the Bill of Rights.

2.2 Threats to rights and liberties

The issue of the lack of clearly defined citizens' rights became more prominent under the governments of Margaret Thatcher and Tony Blair, particularly at the time of the latter's legislation dealing with terrorist threats. In several areas what had been seen as traditional 'rights' appeared to be under threat:

The right to silence

There was uncertainty about how secure the citizen's right to remain silent after arrest was, and whether it actually was a 'right'.

Freedom of the press

There was a strong feeling that the Official Secrets Act prevented the press and other media from doing their 'duty' in checking the government. There was also concern that the rich and powerful, such as the newspaper owner Robert Maxwell and the Conservative politician Jeffrey Archer, could use the threat of libel and slander actions to stop unfavourable (but true) items being published about them.

Freedom to broadcast

The government was able to ban radio or television programmes that it thought might damage state security (but might also reveal its own incompetence). It also prevented broadcasters from having representatives of Sinn Fein, one of the main nationalist parties in Northern Ireland, speaking on television and radio during the Northern Ireland 'troubles'.

The right to privacy

Many 'public' figures, including the royal family, resented the frequent intrusions, photographs and comments about them in the media, sometimes featuring them in very unflattering situations. At the same time, legislation was passed that gave the police and the security services much easier access to telephone conversations.

Freedom of information

Citizens did not have access to information held about them, such as medical records (or UCAS references!), or information about public figures, such as MPs' expenses.

Further concerns arose as a result of the 'anti-terror' legislation following the 9/11 terrorist attacks and the London Underground suicide bombings, such as:

- free speech — the growing use of legal injunctions to muzzle the press and individuals
- the right to protest — where and when there could be public protest
- surveillance — the growing use of CCTV as well as the use by police of cameras at protest meetings
- detention without trial — detaining people suspected of terrorist involvement without charge (the Belmarsh cases are an example of this)
- extradition — allowing UK citizens to be extradited to the USA on limited evidence
- torture — the allegations that the UK security services colluded in the use of torture by other countries on terrorism suspects

Liberties: the simplest definition of liberties is the kind of actions that are considered acceptable by the society you live in. In the UK anyone over the age of 18 is seen to have the 'liberty' to choose who they wish to marry as well as the 'liberty' to remain unmarried.

Always differentiate between a 'right' and a 'liberty'.

Analyse how serious a threat to traditional liberties this legislation is.

Note that civil liberties were a part of the Conservative–Liberal Democrat coalition agreement.

Obviously you need to be able to debate the extent to which the needs of public security should be more important than the need for liberty.

2.3 The European Convention on Human Rights

Many argue that the greatest constitutional change that the Labour government elected in 1997 brought about is the full acceptance of the European Convention on Human Rights and its incorporation into the law of the land. Critics see this acceptance, which was implemented through the Human Rights Act of 1998, as an important loss of national sovereignty, as the UK's judges and Parliament are now bound by it. This Act has largely ended the pressure for a bill of rights for the UK (similar to the clearly listed rights of a US citizen laid out in the US constitution).

The main terms of the convention are:
- the right to life
- freedom from torture
- the right to liberty and security of person
- the right to a fair trial by an impartial tribunal
- the right to respect for private and family life, home and correspondence
- freedom of thought and expression
- the right to an effective remedy against authority, such as a government
- freedom from discrimination

There are also some additions, known as protocols. The main ones are:
- the right to education
- the right to take part in free elections with a secret ballot

This convention, together with the UK's obedience to decisions made by the European Court of Human Rights, has had a major impact on the rights and liberties of citizens in the UK. It has ensured that women workers get equal pay for equal work and have the same retirement age as men. It has affected the way in which police may interrogate suspects and the procedures for expelling or suspending students from school.

The convention is of huge importance, and it will take some years before the full implications are realised. Newspaper editors, while delighted about the 'freedom of expression' part of the convention, are much less enthusiastic about the right to privacy, which they feel might limit their ability to investigate politicians such as Peter Mandelson, Jonathan Aitken and Jeffrey Archer in the way that they did, and to expose their failings. It might also limit their ability to write endlessly about celebrities and their private lives.

2.4 The European Court of Human Rights

If UK citizens feel that any of their rights under the European Convention of Human Rights have been violated, they are fully entitled to take the issue to the European Court of Human Rights if they cannot get redress in the UK's courts. This has happened frequently in the past, and in several cases the European Court of Human Rights has ruled that an action of the UK government was 'illegal'. Examples of this are:

Get your own recent examples of the European Court of Human Rights at work; its website is easy to use.

- the European Court's ruling to stop corporal punishment in UK schools although the UK government had permitted it
- the European Court's ruling that particular methods used by the UK government in Northern Ireland to interrogate IRA suspects were 'torture' and had to be stopped
- the issues of whether prisoners in UK jails could have access to artificial insemination by donor while in jail
- rulings on trade union membership — when a trade union tried to expel members who joined the BNP, its action was declared illegal
- who had, and who did not have, access to social housing
- the rights of asylum seekers
- the rights of gypsies and travellers
- early release of prisoners

Another vital change brought in by the Labour government in 2000 is the Freedom of Information Act, which led to huge changes. Before the Act, all information held by public bodies was automatically secret and inaccessible unless specified otherwise. Since the Act, all information is available unless specified otherwise. It was this Act which enabled a journalist to force Parliament to release details of all MPs' and peers' expenses, with huge political consequences.

3 The defence of rights and liberties in the UK

Candidates need to know the main ways in which a citizen who has had one of his or her 'rights', such as freedom of expression, violated can exercise that right freely and, if necessary, can claim compensation for that violation.

3.1 The role of the judiciary in the defence of rights and liberties

The principal defenders of citizens' rights are the courts of law. If a citizen feels that a policewoman has exceeded her authority and detained them for too long, or an editor feels that he is being prevented from publishing an article critical of a minister, they can go to court.

It is possible for a judge to declare that the action of the policewoman was wrong, or that the article should be published. If the citizen does not like the ruling of the UK judge, he or she can appeal to the European Court of Human Rights — and if that court decides that the judge was wrong, and the citizen's rights were violated, it can overturn the judge's ruling, and UK courts have to obey that decision.

The role of the judges is vital here. Two examples are as follows:
- A judge ruled that an operation to separate Siamese twins could go ahead, even though it would certainly lead to the death of one of them. The judge had to consider the rights and wishes of the parents, who opposed the operation, the rights of the twin who might live, and the rights of the twin who would die.
- Judges had to decide whether farmers had the 'right' to resist government agricultural officials coming onto their land to slaughter animals possibly infected with foot-and-mouth disease.

Get your own recent examples of the courts at work here; the 'Liberty' website is a good starting point.

There is always a concern that the process can be slow and very expensive, and this deters many individuals. Pursuing a case right through to the European Court of Human Rights can take several years, and the costs can run well into six or seven figures.

3.2 The role of Parliament

Another possible defender of the rights of the citizen is Parliament. Constituents have a right to see their MP, either in Westminster or in the MP's 'surgery' in their constituency. MPs do not have extensive powers individually, but they do have some ways to protect people's rights:

- MPs can write directly to a minister or a government department, agency or quango. It is expected that an MP's complaint will be taken seriously and replied to. Many minor issues, such as the non-payment of money owed to citizens by HM Revenue and Customs, or disability pensions, are dealt with effectively at this level.
- They can question a minister orally at Question Time or put down a written question. The latter tends to be more effective, particularly in miscarriage of justice cases.
- They can raise the matter as an adjournment debate at the end of a parliamentary day. This tends to be most effective when dealing with issues affecting groups of constituents — consider, for example, the way in which MPs from rural constituencies used it to protect farmers in the foot-and-mouth crisis.
- They can refer a matter to the ombudsman or a parliamentary select committee. The ombudsman (the parliamentary commissioner for administration) does have some investigative powers.

On the whole, however, the scope for MPs is fairly limited, unless they are part of a wider campaign. The example of Chris Mullin MP and the wrongful conviction of the Birmingham Six shows this.

3.3 The role of the media

Sympathetic and widespread coverage by the media can also help to defend citizens' rights. Two good examples were sympathetic media coverage of the campaign to increase old age pensions and the way in which the media covered Joanna Lumley's campaign to gain UK residence rights for Gurkhas.

3.4 Administrative tribunals

These are independent bodies, set up by government, designed to deal with specific grievances that a citizen may have against a government department or an employer. They are free, impartial and relatively quick. They cover areas such as tax, pensions, compensation for property being taken over to build motorways, unfair dismissal at work, denial of equal opportunities, and racial discrimination. Citizens' Advice Bureaus in most towns will help people to access these tribunals — they tend to know more about these things even than MPs.

If, for example, a citizen feels that she has not been fairly compensated by government for having a motorway put through her land, she can appeal to the

relevant administrative tribunal. It is chaired by an independent lawyer, and will have two specialists in land values/property on it, as well as two local 'lay' people, who are chosen for their common sense and good judgement rather than for any specialist knowledge.

The citizen makes her case before it, assisted by a 'friend' or lawyer if she wishes. The relevant government department's official replies — the reply must be in non-technical language — and then the tribunal makes its decision. It can order compensation to be paid if it considers this appropriate. There is, of course, a right of appeal to the courts if the citizen is unhappy with the decision.

The biggest area of growth for administrative tribunals now lies with those who feel they have been subjected to discrimination at work on grounds of race or sex, or have been unfairly dismissed by an employer.

> Always think about the effectiveness and accessibility of the different ways in which grievances can be redressed.

3.5 Public inquiries

Citizens unhappy with the actions of government or other bodies such as the police or railways can pressurise government directly for a public inquiry. Good examples of this are the Lawrence Inquiry into the way in which the police dealt with the murder of Stephen Lawrence, and the public inquiry into the death of Dr David Kelly. Another example is the inquiry led by a well-known lawyer, Ian Kennedy, into the number of babies who had died after heart surgery in a Bristol hospital. Inquiries may recommend action, but there is no requirement on government to implement their recommendations. The Chilcot Inquiry into the Iraq war is another example worth noting.

3.6 The role of the local councillor

Citizens who have a grievance that comes under the jurisdiction of the local council — in areas such as education, planning and housing — can approach their local councillor in the same way as they would their MP on national matters. There is also access to the local government ombudsman. Local councillors have influence, but lack of public awareness of what a council (or councillor) can and cannot do, means limited use is made of them.

3.7 The role of pressure groups

These are playing an increasing role in enabling individual citizens or groups of citizens to gain redress of grievances or to uphold their rights. There are many examples, ranging from those who form a pressure group to stop a motorway crossing their land (e.g. the building of the M40 north of Oxford) to the group of concerned and distressed parents in the Bristol area who believed that their babies had died unnecessarily through bungled heart surgery. The latter managed to get a public inquiry (see above), compensation and the dismissal of the surgeons involved.